BEACHCOMBING
the Atlantic Coast

Peggy Kochanoff

Mountain Press Publishing Company
Missoula, Montana
1997

To Stan, Jim, and Tom

*Many thanks to Jim Kochanoff for typing and computer work
and to Peggy Hamilton for proofreading the manuscript.*

Cover drawing © 1997 Peggy Kochanoff

Cover drawing colorized by Ed Jenne

Library of Congress Cataloging-in-Publication Data

Kochanoff, Peggy, 1943-
    Beachcombing the Atlantic Coast / Peggy Kochanoff.
      p.   cm.
    Includes bibliographical references (p.   ) and index.
    ISBN 0-87842-345-1 (pbk.)
    1. Seashore biology—Atlantic Coast (U.S.)   2. Beachcombing—
Atlantic Coast (U.S.)   I. Title.
QH92.2.K63   1997
574.909'46—dc20   96-46134
                                                    CIP

Printed in the United States of America

Mountain Press Publishing Company
P.O. Box 2399 • Missoula, MT 59806
(406) 728-1900 • Fax (406) 728-1635

Contents

INTRODUCTION   1
  Distribution and Currents   2
  Tides   2
  Seashore Types   4
    Rocky Coasts *4*
    Sandy Coasts *4*
    Salt Marshes *5*
    Tide Pools *5*

ANIMALS   13
  Sponges   15
    Finger Sponge *16*
  Coelenterates   17
    Portuguese Man-of-War *18*
    Moon Jellyfish *20*
    Sea Anemone *21*
    Coral *22*
  Worms   23
    Lugworm *24*
    Clam Worm *25*
  Echinoderms   26
    Green Sea Urchin *27*
    Eastern Starfish *28*
    Sand Dollar *30*
    Sea Cucumber *31*
  Mollusks   32
    Scallop *33*
    Blue Mussel *34*
    Jingle Shell *36*
    Oyster *37*

Soft-Shell Clam *38*
Northern Quahog *39*
Razor Clam *40*
Limpet *41*
Boat Shell *42*
Periwinkle *42*
Worm Shell *43*
Moon Shell *44*
Knobbed Whelk *45*
Squid *46*

Arthropods   **47**
Lobster *48*
Rock Crab *50*
Fiddler Crab *51*
Hermit Crab *52*
Mole Crab *53*
Horseshoe Crab *54*
Barnacle *56*
Sand Hopper *57*

Fish   **58**
Flounder *59*
Mermaid's Purse and
    Common Skate *60*
Sand Shark *61*
Sea Robin *62*
Striped Blenny *63*
Butterfish *64*
Naked Goby *65*
Cunner *66*

Sea Turtle   **67**
Green Sea Turtle *68*

Sea Mammals   **69**
Humpback Whale *70*
Pilot Whale *72*
Dolphin *73*
Harbor Seal *74*

Birds   **75**
Double-Crested Cormorant *76*
Common Tern *77*
Herring Gull *78*

Red Knot   *79*
Semipalmated Plover   *80*
Black-Bellied Plover   *81*
Least Sandpiper   *82*
Spotted Sandpiper   *83*
Sanderling   *84*
Ruddy Turnstone   *85*
Great Blue Heron   *86*
Atlantic Puffin   *87*

PLANTS   **89**

Seaweeds   **91**
Irish Moss   *92*
Dulse   *93*
Bladder Wrack   *94*
Kelp   *95*
Sea Lettuce   *96*

Flowering Plants   **97**
Dusty Miller   *98*
Beach Pea   *99*
Beach Heath   *100*
Sea Rocket   *101*
Bayberry   *102*
Eelgrass   *103*
Beach Grass   *104*
Cordgrass   *105*
Salt-Marsh Bulrush   *106*
Jointed Glasswort   *107*
Sea Lavender   *108*

Geographic Distribution of Plants and Animals Described in This Book   **111**

Bibliography   **117**

Index   **119**

About the Author   **122**

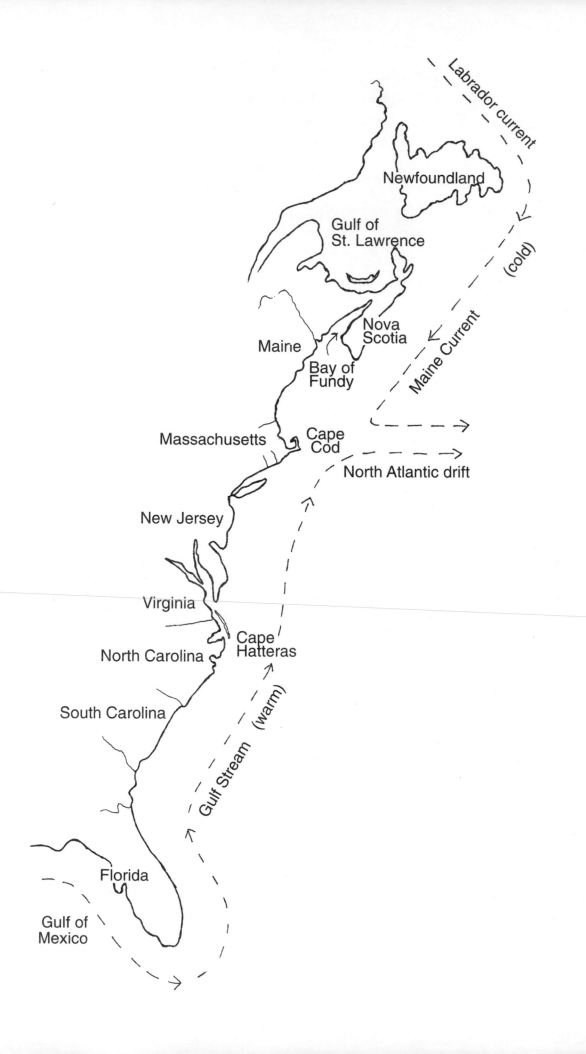

Introduction

Almost all of us have fond memories of summers at the beach—beachcombing for hours, picking up sea urchins and other creatures at low tide, watching shorebirds chase and be chased by the foamy waves, and heading home with a few shells in a pocket. This book is a beginner's guide to the fascinating plants and animals found where land and sea meet—the seashore.

Plants and animals chosen for this book are fairly common, always interesting, and found on a variety of beaches. Most live between the low tide and high tide mark (intertidal zone) or in shallow water below the low tide mark (subtidal zone). A few, such as the humpback whale, might be sighted offshore. Some that dwell offshore might be washed ashore by waves.

The seashore is a diverse environment. Tides continually change the water's edge. Where you found a worm underwater in the morning, you might find a seaweed on dry sand in the afternoon. The many types of seashores—rocky, sandy, marshy, and combinations of each—also provide habitat for a wide variety of flora and fauna.

Please be careful as you beachcomb. Different provinces and states have different regulations about collecting; find out what they are and abide by them. Most parks prohibit removal of *anything*. Most things are more fun to watch in their own habitat anyway. Use common sense and do not disturb endangered plants or animals, nests of birds, and living things in general. If you pick up a living thing to examine it, replace it where you found it and respect its habitat. As you understand and appreciate the animals and plants that make the seashore their home, you will learn how their lives interact in that unique and fragile environment.

Happy beachcombing!

DISTRIBUTION and CURRENTS

Most plants and animals described in this book can be found from the Bay of Fundy to Cape Hatteras, North Carolina. The majority of them also range farther north into the Arctic or south to Florida and the Gulf of Mexico. Some are so well adapted they can exist along most of the Atlantic coast.

Water temperature is a main factor in determining range, and this can vary with the season. Water temperature determines which cold-water larvae can exist in warmer southern waters and which southern species can tolerate winter's cold in the north. The coolness in deep waters can extend ranges farther south. High winds and storms also can extend ranges farther south by transporting creatures on currents or attached to driftwood or seaweed.

Cold waters from the Labrador Current flow as far south as northern Cape Cod. The warm Gulf Stream moves slowly north to about Cape Hatteras, where it veers toward Europe. Cape Cod, where the currents meet, supports many diverse plants and animals because of the temperature range between its north and south shores.

TIDES

Tides are a result of the gravitational pull of the moon and the sun on our oceans. When the moon and sun are in line with the earth, they pull together on the water. At these times, high tides are at their highest and low tides are at their lowest. These extreme tides are called spring tides.

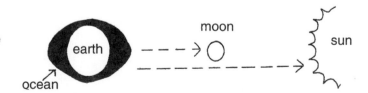

Configuration of the sun, the moon, and the earth that causes spring tides.

When the sun and moon are at right angles to each other, the forces of pull partially cancel each other. A minimum tide change, called a neap tide, results.

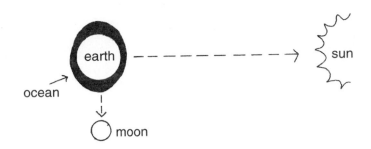

Configuration of the sun,
the moon, and the earth
that causes neap tides.

The moon orbits the earth every 27½ days, changing position daily and rising about fifty minutes later each day. So, at the same point on the earth, the tide changes fifty minutes later each day.

That explains one tide change every day, but most places have two high tides and two low tides each day. The second tide is a result of centrifugal force. The moon is so large and close to the earth that its pull causes the earth and moon to whip around a common center of gravity. This point lies about 100 miles below the earth's surface on the side toward the moon. The farther an object on earth is away from this point, the more it will fly away from the center. Water on the side of the earth away from the moon will pull away from the earth. Tides on one side are primarily gravitational and on the other side are centrifugal.

"Whipping" effect. The X
marks the center of gravity.

The height and the time of the tides can also be complicated by the irregular shape of a coastline. For example, in the Bay of Fundy, where a 45-vertical-foot change in tide is common, water from a large, wide area (the open ocean) is funneled into a narrow, contained area (the Bay of Fundy). An open coast like Cape Cod's has 3-to-4-foot tides. Offshore and onshore winds can also influence the height of the tide.

Tides act as food delivery systems for animals living near shore. The changing tides carry nutrients from deeper water on incoming tides and pull nutrients out of marshes and river mouths on outgoing tides. They also pull out wastes and disperse eggs and young.

Beachcombing is most fun at low tide, so check local tide schedules in the newspaper or pick up a tide table at a marine or fishing shop. The time of low tide will vary a little each day.

SEASHORE TYPES

Seashores come in many types: rocky, sandy, marshy, and combinations of these. The drawings that follow show some of the plants and animals you might find in three coastal habitats. You will not find all of these plants and animals at one time in one place, but it is fun to look for them all.

Rocky Coasts

Rocky coasts are typically rough, jagged cliffs with waves crashing against them. Most plants and animals that live along rocky coasts have some means of clinging to the rocks and resisting the pull of waves. They use suction, glue, or a holdfast to stay on the rocks or hide in protected crevices.

Some plants and animals are exposed to sun and air part of the day; others are always underwater. In a small area, you can see a vertical progression of organisms from ones that need a little moisture, to those that are wet about half of the time, to those that stay wet most of the time and cannot tolerate drying out.

Sandy Coasts

Sand along the Northeast coast is composed primarily of bits of granite and other igneous rocks. South toward Florida, the sand is mainly crushed coral, shells, tiny animals, and skeletons. In damp sand, a film of water around each grain helps hold the grains together and protects them from the grinding action of the waves. Because sand holds it shape when moved, many burrowing animals make their homes on sandy shores. On sandy beaches, marine animals are more likely to have some freedom of movement—they can swim, crawl, wiggle, or walk around—because the waves are less destructive than on rocky beaches and will not sweep them away.

The strand line is a line of debris washed ashore and deposited at the point of high tide. A storm may add debris from far away to the strand line. The wet sand between the strand line and the water's edge is home to many small burrowing creatures.

Sand dunes are part of the sandy coast. They are harsh habitats with hot sun, strong winds, drifting sand, and salt spray. Dunes form where debris accumulates and sand collects around it. As the dune's wind resistance increases, more sand piles up. Plants that grow on the dunes help stabilize them. Certain grasses and other plants, such as beach grass, beach pea, and dusty miller, survive here. In the dunes, watch for insects, spiders, grasshoppers, flies, wasps, and ants. You can also occasionally spot birds, snakes, raccoons, mice, foxes, and other animals in the dunes.

Salt Marshes

Salt marshes are muddy areas characterized by such salt-tolerant grasses as eelgrass, cord grass, salt marsh bulrush, and cattails. Marshes form along coasts where there is protection from the pounding surf. In this calm habitat, clay, silt, and plant debris collect on the marsh's muddy bottom and later build up to form soil and solid land.

Salt marshes produce large amounts of plants that are valuable as food and protection for animals. Marshes are excellent places to view wildlife. Around the marsh, you might see great blue herons, red-winged blackbirds, raccoons, fiddler crabs, marsh periwinkles, and ribbed mussels. You might not want to beachcomb in a salt marsh, though, because it has a lot of sharp grasses and slimy (sometimes smelly) mud.

Tide Pools

Shallow tide pools form along sandy and rocky coastlines. Tide pools are fun because the calm, low water makes it easy to see many things. Most of the plants and animals here need to be covered with water. Many of them are mobile, so watch them scurry around.

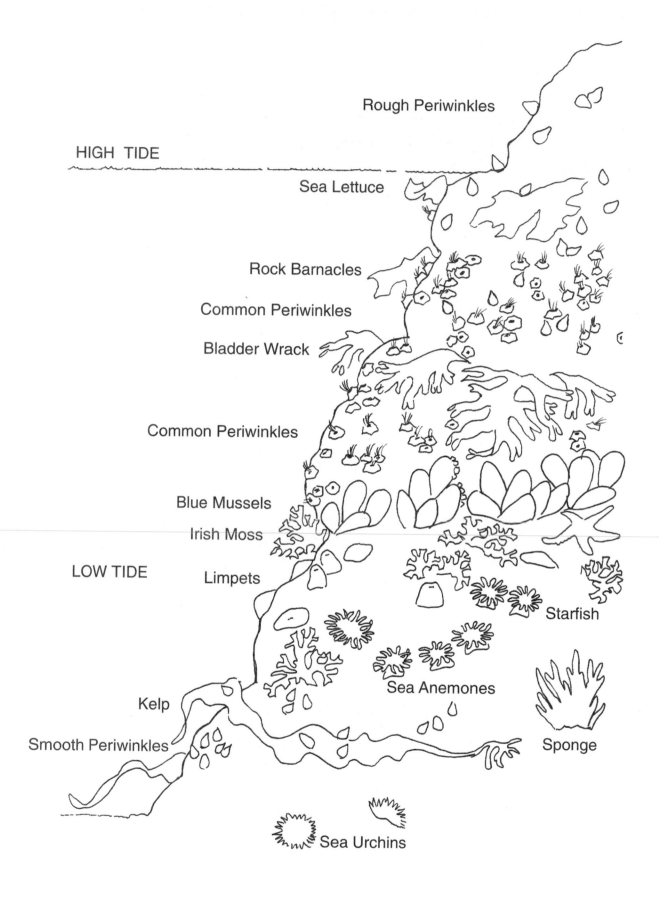

Rough Periwinkles

HIGH TIDE

Sea Lettuce

Rock Barnacles

Common Periwinkles

Bladder Wrack

Common Periwinkles

Blue Mussels

Irish Moss

LOW TIDE

Limpets

Starfish

Sea Anemones

Kelp

Smooth Periwinkles

Sponge

Sea Urchins

ROCKY COAST

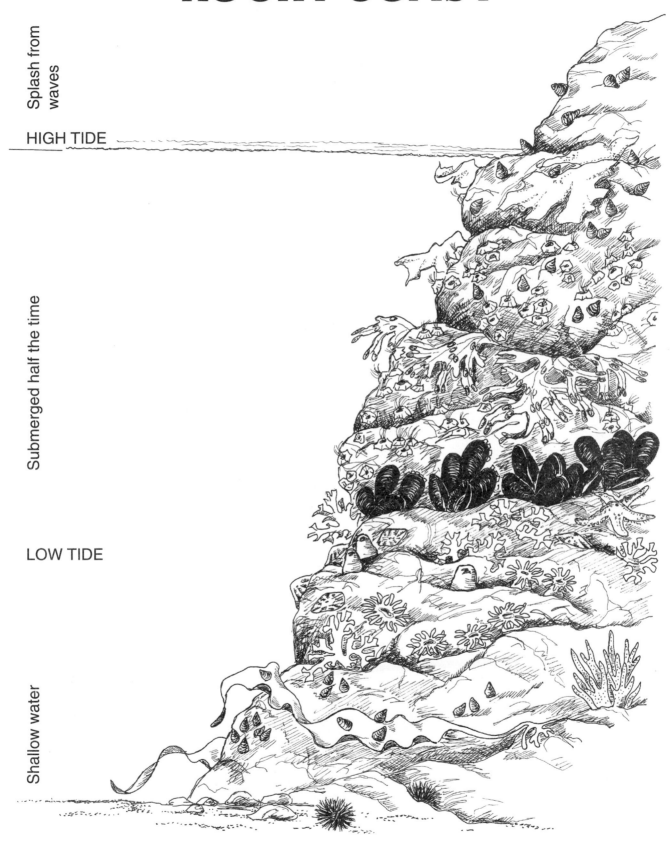

Splash from waves

HIGH TIDE

Submerged half the time

LOW TIDE

Shallow water

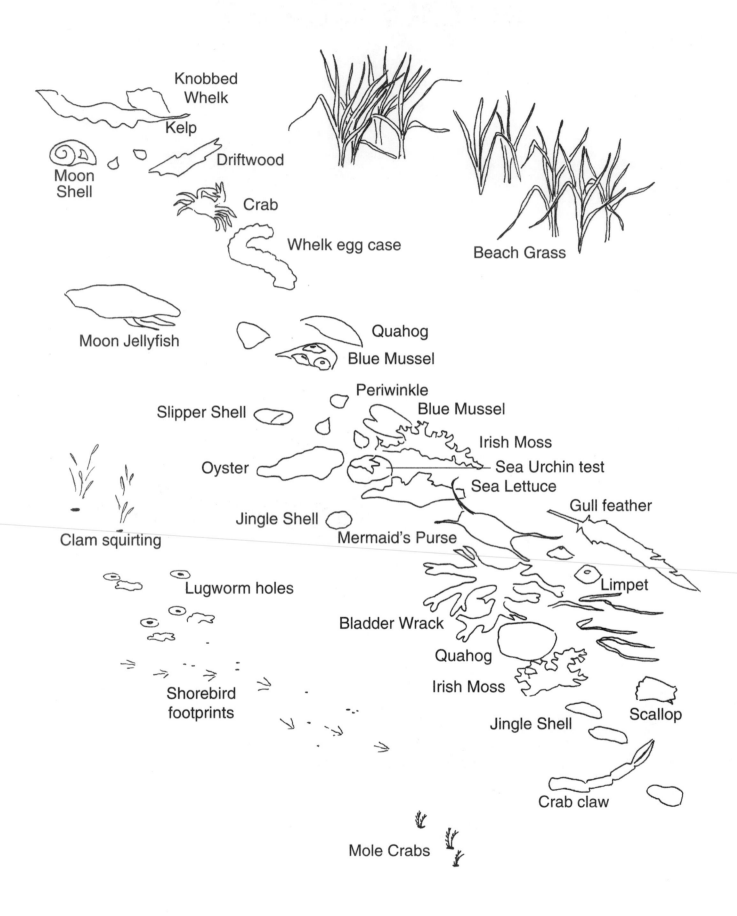

Knobbed Whelk

Kelp

Driftwood

Moon Shell

Crab

Whelk egg case

Beach Grass

Moon Jellyfish

Quahog

Blue Mussel

Periwinkle

Slipper Shell

Blue Mussel

Irish Moss

Oyster

Sea Urchin test

Sea Lettuce

Gull feather

Jingle Shell

Mermaid's Purse

Clam squirting

Limpet

Lugworm holes

Bladder Wrack

Quahog

Irish Moss

Shorebird footprints

Jingle Shell

Scallop

Crab claw

Mole Crabs

STRAND LINE

Eelgrass

Starfish

Knobbed Whelk

Dulse

Horseshoe Crab

Sand Collar

Rock Crab

Clam Worm

Sea Urchin

Hermit Crab

Quahog

Periwinkle

Scallop

Oyster

Starfish

Periwinkle

Kelp

Sand Dollar

Irish Moss

Soft-Shell Clam

Scallop

Starfish

Quahog

Sea
Lettuce

Jingle Shell

Moon Shell

TIDE POOL

ANIMALS

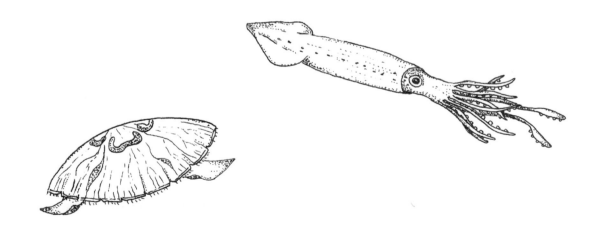

SPONGES

Sponges are the most primitive many-celled animal. They lack organs but have specialized cells for different functions. Water flows through their many holes and is filtered for food.

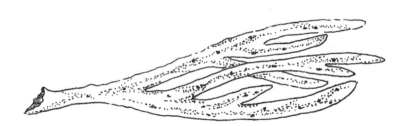

FINGER SPONGE

Haliclona oculata

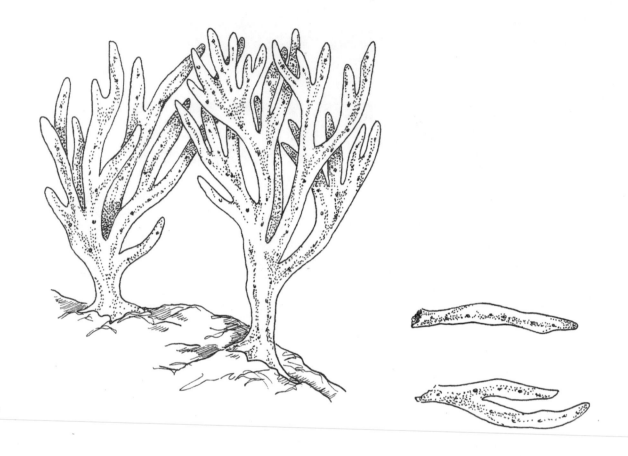

Soft fingerlike pieces of this sponge wash ashore after storms. The main animal is light yellow-brown and has many branched, erect arms. A single stalk attaches itself to rocks, pilings, or shells, where it grows and adds arms. The finger sponge has no mouth, but water flows through many tiny pores. The sponge filters microscopic food from the water before it flows out through other pores.

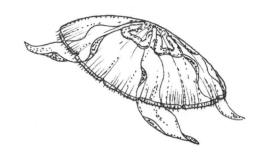

COELENTERATES

Coelenterates are animals that lack shells or true skeletons. Their simple bodies have a single opening for food, and their tentacles carry stinging cells.

PORTUGUESE MAN-OF-WAR

Physalia physalia

This striking animal got its name when it was first sighted in Portugal. It resembles a man-of-war ship under sail.

Each man-of-war is actually a colony of hundreds of animals, or polyps, living together. The individual animals are modified to do different jobs. There are four specialized cell types in the colony. Some polyps reproduce. Others have tentacles that catch food. Still others digest food. All are attached to a gas-filled float, or bubble, that catches the wind. Because the man-of-war goes where the wind blows the float, storms may blow these jellyfish-like animals onto northern beaches far from their normal warm-water homes.

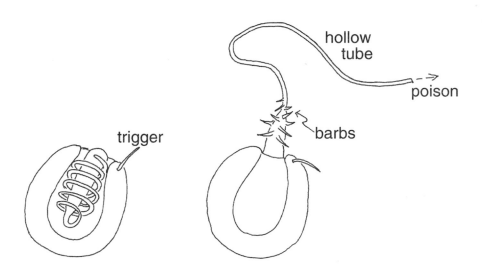

Below the beautiful pink and lavender bubble (3 to 12 inches long) you see floating on the surface are many stinging tentacles up to 50 feet long. When a tentacle is touched, the stinging cells (called nematocysts) fire little darts that release a powerful poison that will paralyze fish. Strangely, the poison is not toxic to loggerhead turtles or fish of the genus *Nomeus,* which often live among the tentacles. If you touch the tentacles of a Portuguese man-of-war, the poison will severely burn or blister your skin, even if the animal is dead. So beware! Some beaches are closed when Portuguese man-of-war are around.

MOON JELLYFISH

Aurelia aurita

In spite of its name, the moon jellyfish is not a true fish but a simple creature with a jellylike substance between an inner and outer wall of cells. It is shaped like an upside-down sea anemone. It pulsates along the water, its movements similar to an umbrella opening and closing, but is at the mercy of the currents. The tentacles have tiny stinging cells that paralyze fish. When a tentacle touches a fish, it shoots out a small dart with a hollow thread. Poison flows through the hollow thread to the fish. Even when a jellyfish is dead on the beach, its tentacles can still sting. This species is less venomous than others, but its sting might give you an itchy rash.

An adult moon jellyfish eats plankton that it catches on sticky barbs on its "umbrella" and scrapes off with its arms. The four rings on top of the umbrella are reproductive organs. In young, the rings are white. On adult males, the  rings turn yellow, yellow brown, or rose. On adult females, the rings turn yellow, pink, or violet. The rest of the jellyfish is transparent or pinkish.

SEA ANEMONE

Northern Red Anemone *Tealia felina*

Despite their beautiful flowerlike appearance, sea anemones are animals. Anemones come in a rainbow of colors. The northern red anemone is red, sometimes with green spots. The anemone's one hundred or so petal-like tentacles sting prey that venture too close, then sweep the victims into the anemone's mouth. The anemone sucks food into its stomach, where strong enzymes can digest a small crab in five minutes.

When disturbed, the anemone draws its tentacles inward, leaving behind a wrinkled blob of jelly. The anemone's sting is not poisonous to humans.

Look for anemones near the low-tide mark, where they attach themselves to rocks, sand, seaweeds, and wood. They may move slightly from day to day.

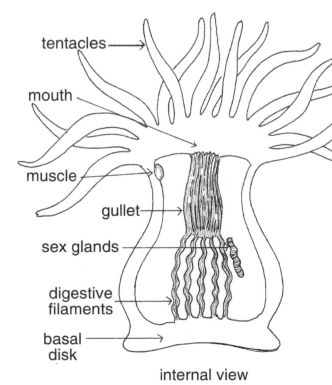

tentacles

mouth

muscle

gullet

sex glands

digestive filaments

basal disk

internal view

CORAL

Northern Stony Coral *Astrangia danae*

The small hard pieces of coral you find washed up on shore are limestone skeletons of colonies of small, live animals. In spite of their plantlike appearance, corals are animals. Free-swimming coral larvae settle on rocks and shells and begin secreting calcium carbonate (the main component of limestone) cups. In each 1/4-inch-wide cup is a small polyp, similar to a sea anemone. The polyp looks like a sac with a mouth fringed by tentacles. These tentacles sweep microscopic food into the polyp's mouth and stun prey with stinging cells. The polyps—typically living in colonies of about thirty in this species—can retract into their stony cups. Free-swimming larvae hatch from fertilized eggs. They eventually settle on a surface and secrete calcium carbonate. Established polyps can also reproduce asexually by budding—producing an outgrowth that forms a new organism.

Most coral live in warm southern waters, where they form large reefs, but a few, like this one, grow in cool waters as far north as Cape Cod. The southern reefs are the hard limestone skeletons left after the polyps die. Reefs form only in water warmer than 64° Fahrenheit (18° Celsius) and less than 280 feet deep. Unfortunately, some reefs are dying due to pollution, siltation, dragging of nets, collectors, and careless divers. Silt clogs the polyps so they cannot filter food. Large nets dragged over a coral reef can break off pieces of coral, damaging the reef. Careless divers also break pieces off with their feet, flippers, hands, and knives.

mouth

tentacles

limestone base→

single polyp

WORMS

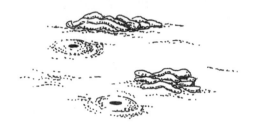

Worms have long tubular or leech-shaped bodies.
Some are smooth, others have many segments.

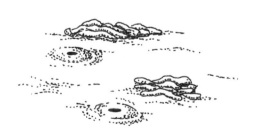

LUGWORM

Arenicola cristata

You may not see lugworms, but you will probably see their homes. Lugworms build U-shaped burrows in wet sand, using mucous to plaster the sides to prevent collapse. The opening at the burrow's mouth is a funnel-shaped depression where the lugworm takes in mud and sand and removes any organic matter. Like earthworms, lugworms excrete the nonedible sand and other material out the other end of the burrow. Look for small mounds of sand coils marking the "tail end" of the burrow.

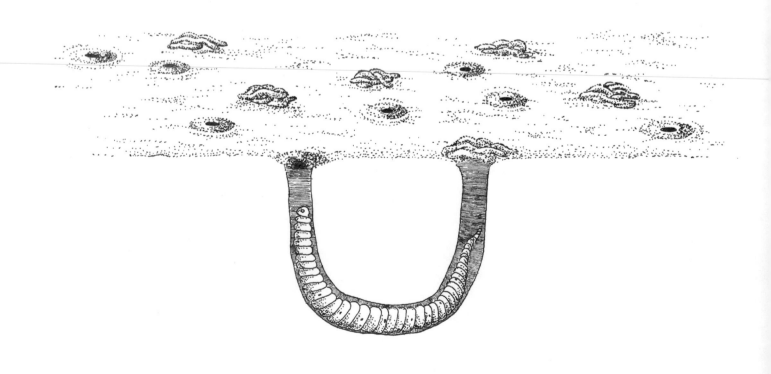

CLAM WORM

Nereis virens

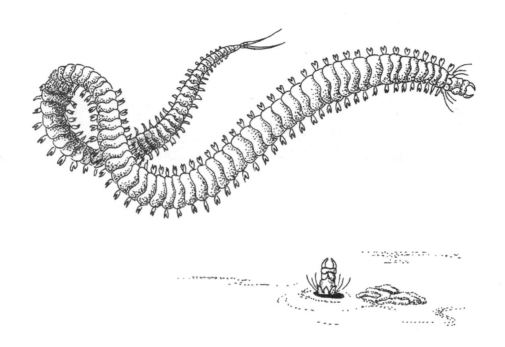

These aggressive animals have strong sharp jaws for catching prey—or giving your finger a nip (though it doesn't really hurt). When hunting, the clam worm can withdraw and conceal its jaws from unsuspecting prey. These worms ingest sand and mud looking for microorganisms. In the process, they also take in pollutants, which become concentrated in their bodies. When the worms are eaten by other animals, they pass the pollution on.

Look for the bright blue green color of the male or the orange red of the female. Paddles along the length of the worm's body enable it to swim well. With sticky fluid, the worms form tubes in mud or sand and hide in these burrows during the day. If you take a flashlight to the beach at night, you might glimpse clam worms hunting.

ECHINODERMS

Spiny skin covers echinoderms. These animals are usually round, have body parts in groups of five, and move with tiny tube feet.

GREEN SEA URCHIN

Strongylocentrotus droebachiensis

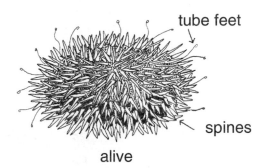

tube feet

spines

alive

dead

Green sea urchins typically live in calm waters. Fierce spines, each moveable on a ball-and-socket joint, cover these olive green creatures. In spite of their spiny exterior, sea urchins are eaten by many fish, starfish, and Pacific sea otters. Urchins use long tube feet that stick out beyond the spines for breathing, sensory reception, seizing food, and anchoring themselves to rocks. Sea urchins have five strong teeth on their undersides, which grow throughout their life. The teeth scrape and grind seaweed and other food.

When urchins die, the spines fall off, leaving behind a bumpy skeleton called a test. The bumps are the knobs on which the spines moved within their joints. Tiny pores visible on the hard skeleton are where tube feet extended when the urchin was alive. Look for live urchins in tide pools and for whole or broken tests and sea urchin spines along the strand line of sandy beaches.

five bottom teeth

EASTERN STARFISH

Asterias forbesi

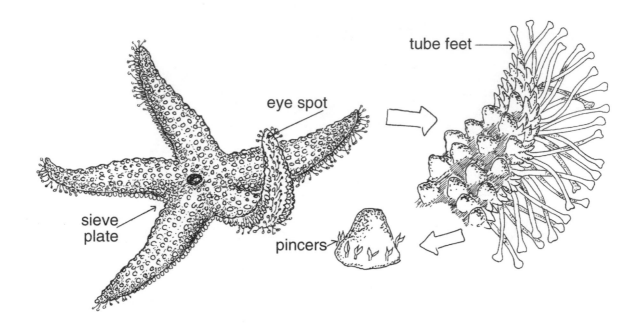

The eastern starfish has five arms, under which are hundreds of small tubelike feet that end in suckers. With the suckers, the starfish clings with surprising strength to rocks, shells, and wood. At the tip of each arm is a small reddish eyespot that can detect light and dark. With a magnifying glass you can see tiny pincers around the bony lumps on the starfish's skin. They help keep algae and other debris from settling on the skin.

If a starfish's arm is cut off, it can grow another one in about a year. If a piece of the starfish has some of the central disk (the central part of the starfish), it can regenerate a new starfish. In years gone by, fishermen, worried that starfish were eating all the shellfish, would cut starfish into pieces and throw them back into the water. Instead of killing the starfish, the fishermen were increasing the numbers.

Water enters the eastern starfish's internal system through the red spot, called the sieve plate, on the animal's top side. Inside are many connected water-filled canals. Tube feet lengthen or contract as muscles pump seawater in and out through interconnected channels in the body.

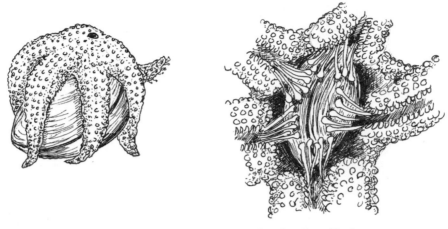

tube feet pull clam open

When it catches prey, perhaps a clam, the starfish wraps its arms around the victim. Its tube feet pull and pull until the clam's muscle tires and the shell opens a crack. Quickly, the starfish pushes its stomach out through its mouth (on the bottom side) and into the clam. The stomach surrounds the clam's body, secretes digestive enzymes, and absorbs the mixture.

SAND DOLLAR

Echinarachnius parma

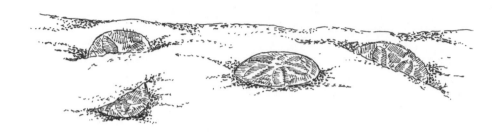

Sand dollars are related to sea urchins, but with reduced and flattened spines. These unusual round animals burrow in sandbars in shallow water. Small moveable tube feet and velvety spines cover both sides. With the tube feet, the sand dollar slowly moves through the sand, trapping microorganisms and pushing them to its mouth, located in the center of the bottom side. Larger tube feet on top, in the star shape, are used like gills for breathing.

When alive, sand dollars are reddish brown or purple. The white sand dollars you find on the beach are the skeletons of the dead animals. After sand dollars die, they fade, the velvet spines and the tube feet fall off, and holes often develop—but they are still pretty treasures in the sand.

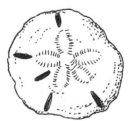

Sand dollar skeleton

SEA CUCUMBER

Orange-Footed Cucumber *Cucumaria frondosa*

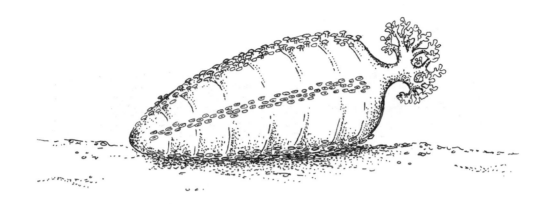

This strange cucumber-shaped animal is reddish brown as an adult, with orange-tipped tube feet in five bands that run the length of its body. Bushy-tipped tentacles surround its mouth. By contracting its muscles, the sea cucumber slowly creeps along the seafloor. Its tube feet cling tightly to rocks and seaweed. When annoyed, the sea cucumber can eject its inner organs to scare an attacker and grow new ones later. If accidentally out of water, this remarkable animal can change shape into a flabby ball to prevent drying out.

MOLLUSKS

A sheet of soft tissue, called the mantle, covers most of a mollusk's body. The mantle secretes a hard shell, which is usually external but can be internal. Mollusks typically creep along the seafloor on a muscular foot.

SCALLOP

Atlantic Bay Scallop   *Argopecten irradians*

The beautifully shaped scallop has about twenty elevated ribs and small "wings" on each side at the hinge. The ribs give the shell great strength. Scallops have a unique way of moving. A strong muscle claps the two shells together, forcing water out in one direction and propelling the scallop forward in the other direction. Their movements are erratic and jerky.

ribs
eyes
tentacles
gills

Rows of tiny blue eyes ring the edge of the mantle. Each eye—complete with a lens, retina, and optic nerve—can detect light, dark, and movement but not actual forms. This "vision" is a great help in escaping enemies. Tentacles located between the eyes are sensitive to touch and help capture microorganisms.

BLUE MUSSEL

Mytilus edulis

byssus

Mussels, with their glossy, blue black shells, cling to rocks and wooden pilings, often in large numbers. They attach to a surface using a tough thread, called a byssus, that they eject from the foot as a sticky fluid that hardens. To change position, a mussel just cuts the threads and moves on. Siphons suck water into the gills, which filter it for microorganisms. While filtering, a mussel may also ingest water pollutants, which become concentrated in the animal.

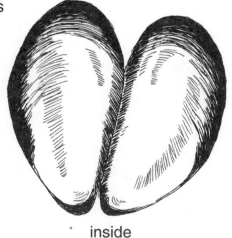

Mussel shells

outside

inside

JINGLE SHELL

Anomia simplex

A favorite collectible, jingle shells are thin, glossy, and irregularly shaped. They come in many colors, including white, yellow, orange, and even gray and black. Strung on a string as a wind chime or a necklace, these shells make a delightful jingling sound.

When the free-swimming larvae settle, they permanently attach themselves to rocks, shells, or pilings. The bottom shell, smaller and flatter than the top shell, has a hole through which the tough byssal threads pass to fasten the shell to

the surface. The larger, more hollowed upper shell is the one you will most likely find washed ashore.

OYSTER

Crassostrea virginica

The oyster's rough outer shell hides a smooth, iridescent mollusk inside. The irregular, grayish white shells grow to 15 inches long. The lower half is flatter than the upper half. Oysters attach themselves to rocks, pilings, and other objects using cement secreted by the mantle. The purple spot on the inside of the shell is a scar from the muscle attachment.

Oyster shell

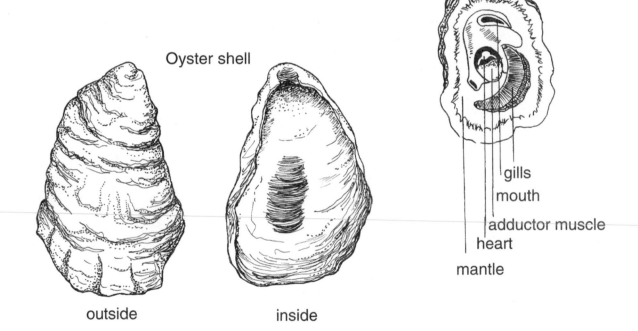

outside   inside

gills
mouth
adductor muscle
heart
mantle

Oysters release millions of eggs into the water every year, during spring and summer when the water is about 80° F. The free-swimming larvae that hatch from the eggs and escape being eaten settle on rocks, wood, or shells and continue to grow for about ten years.

Pearl oysters are a different type of oyster that live in tropical seas. When an irritating object, such as a sand grain, lodges in the mantle, the oyster covers it with layers of a pearly substance. Over years this becomes a pearl.

SOFT-SHELL CLAM

Mya arenaria

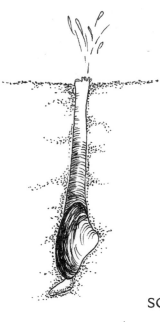

As you walk along a wet sandy beach or mudflat, watch for jets of water squirting several inches high out of the sand or mud. These jets of water tell you that soft-shell clams lie beneath the surface there. When they feel the vibration of your step, the clams eject water through fleshy tubes called siphons so they can draw them back into their shells. Also known as long-necked clams, they can dig as deep as 10 or 12 inches—and stretch their siphons that distance back to the surface. Soft-shell clams are popular for eating, but like other filter feeders they may filter pollutants into their bodies.

NORTHERN QUAHOG
Mercenaria mercenaria

Quahogs have large, thick shells with beautiful shades of purple inside. Indians made beads from pieces of purple shell, which they used in necklaces and wampum belts.

Quahogs have two fleshy tubes, called siphons. The clams suck water into their gills through one siphon. The gills filter microorganisms and oxygen for the clam, then push water and wastes out the other siphon. The quahog's siphons are shorter than those of the soft-shelled clam, so quahogs live in shallower burrows. To dig, the quahog swells its foot with fluid. This enlarges the hole. As the foot shrinks, the clam can move into the space. When the tide goes out, the clam pulls in its foot and siphon and tightly closes its shell until the next high tide brings water—and food—back to the quahog's home.

RAZOR CLAM

Enis directus

Like other clams, razor clams have two shells held together by a strong muscle. The razor clam's shells are 6 to 7 inches long and narrow, like an old-fashioned straight razor. With their strong muscular foot and streamlined shape, they can dig themselves vertically into the sand with amazing speed—half their length per second. They move so fast that it is hard to dig one up with your hands. You might even see a razor clam swimming erratically through the water. Fully extended, the razor clam's foot can be as long as the shell. Short siphons stick out of the sand and draw in water to filter microorganisms.

LIMPET

Tortoise-Shell Limpet *Notoacmaea testudinalis*

Even strong waves almost never dislodge limpets from their rock homes. The limpet's foot creates extremely strong suction, and the low, cone shape of the shells offers little for the waves to grab. These creatures are snails that have lost their spirals. At high tide they slowly move around in their own area eating algae, scraping it off the rocks with their file-like tongues. When the tide goes out, they crawl back to their individual depressions that they have scraped into the rocks.

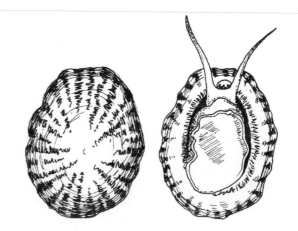

BOAT SHELL

Crepidula fornicata

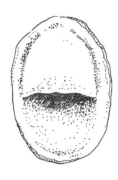  

Have you ever sailed these shells, also called slipper shells, as tiny boats in sandbar streams?

These creatures have no operculum, or lid that closes, so the horizontal shelf inside the shell keeps digestive organs in place and provides protection. Boat shells eat microscopic plants and animals by filtering water containing them through their gills. What they do not eat they store in a pouch until they are hungry again.

Look for boat shells attached by suction to each other, forming stacks ten to thirteen shells high. Each stack is a consecutive generation with the smallest and sexually immature on top. They start out as males, and as they mature, they become bisexual, then female. So, the largest female is on the bottom, and the youngest male is on the top. The males on top fertilize the bisexual individuals below. The bisexuals, in turn, fertilize each other and the females on the bottom. The timing of the sex changes is influenced by water temperature, available food, and chemical scents released by the females.

41

PERIWINKLE

Littorina littorea

Look for these small snail-like shells clinging by the hundreds to seaweed and rocks. The drab olive brown to black shells are 1 to 1½ inches long. Using sandpaper-like tongues called radula, they graze on algae found on rocks. Periwinkles move using a muscular, fleshy foot. A trap door, called an operculum, made of tough protein can seal the shell up tight to protect the animal from predators or from drying out.

Periwinkle shells

fleshy foot

You might find three types of periwinkles along this coast, each in a different habitat. Rough periwinkles spend most of their time out of water but where they are splashed by high waves. Rough periwinkles will drown if covered by water for long. Common periwinkles live where they are exposed to air when the tide goes out twice a day. They can spend much time out of water but must be in the sea to release their sperm and eggs. Smooth periwinkles remain completely in water except during the lowest tides.

WORM SHELL

Vermicularia spirata

Mollusks, not worms, live inside these unusual spiraling shells. The animals inside have elongate, cream-colored bodies with tentacles, eyes, and rough tongues. The worm shell attaches to other shells, and its tentacles sweep food into the animal's mouth. If threatened, the mollusk retreats deep into its shell, closing the open end behind it.

When the animals are young, the shells form tight coils. As the animals get older, the tubes spiral less tightly and more irregularly. Sometimes several grow together in a tangled mass.

MOON SHELL

Northern Moon Shell   *Lunatia heros*

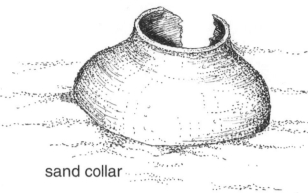

sand collar

Beautifully smooth and whorled moon shells are easy to identify. They come in shades of gray and tan and can reach 4 inches long. The moon shell has an enormous fleshy foot that expands to move the animal about in search of food and contracts completely into the shell when disturbed. A horny trap door, called an operculum, shuts after the moon shell draws its foot inside, protecting the animal from harm.

The moon shell uses its foot to engulf other mollusks, its main prey. Using a filelike tongue and acid produced from a gland, the moon shell bores a hole into its victim's shell. The moon shell inserts its snout in the hole and sucks up the victim's body.

Moon shells lay their eggs in a sand-covered, jellylike ring. As adults crawl away, the circle breaks, forming what looks like a collar. Babies develop inside the collar and then crawl away. It is fun to try to preserve the delicate collar with a coating of nail polish before it dries completely and crumbles.

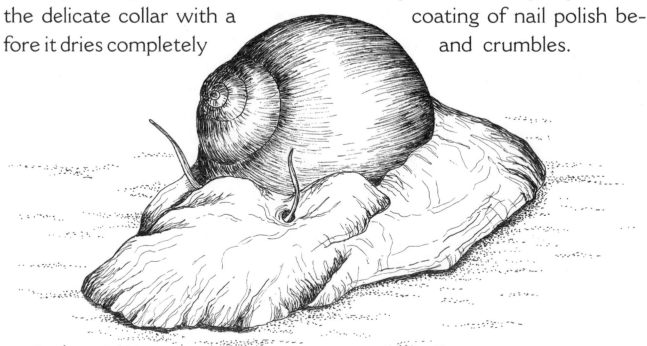

KNOBBED WHELK

Busycon carica

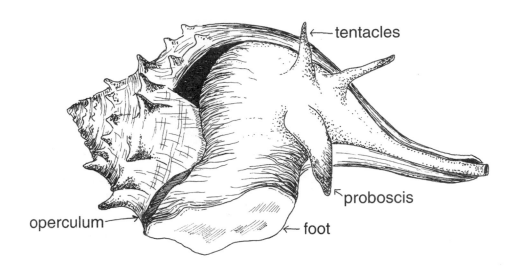

There are many types of whelks, but the knobbed whelk has characteristic bumps or knobs on the shell whorls. The soft-bodied animals inside these 5-to-9-inch-long shells eat other shellfish by drilling through the victim's shell with a sandpaper-like tongue in the snout, or proboscis. The whelk then sucks out the victim's body fluid.

The knobbed whelk's tentacles have simple eyes at the ends to detect light. When the animals withdraw inside the shell, the trap door, or operculum, shuts the shell up tight. Whelks lay long strips of horny egg cases. You might find them washed ashore. Tiny whelks live inside the unopened circular cases.

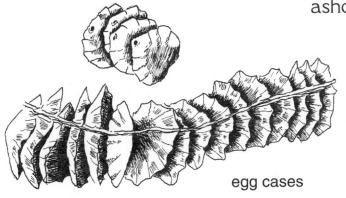

egg cases

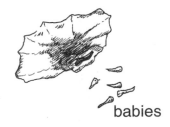

babies

45

SQUID

Long-Finned Squid *Loligo pealei*

These pretty, soft-bodied animals swim by squirting water out one end—which shoots them backward at up to 20 miles per hour! If attacked, squid protect themselves by ejecting dark ink either as a screen so they escape or as a blob for the enemy to attack. Squid can also change their muted color to blend into the background. Suction cups cover the squid's ten food-gathering arms. Two arms are longer than the others and have flattened ends. The animal's mouth has a strong parrotlike beak that easily bites the backs of fish it catches. Large eyes similar to mammal eyes provide keen eyesight.

After mating, squid lay eggs in long strings of foul-tasting jelly. Adults attach these strings to rocks, weeds, or the bottom, where they stay until the young hatch.

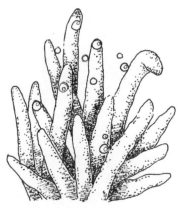

egg cases

ARTHROPODS

Arthropods have jointed legs and a
hard external skeleton.

LOBSTER

Homarus americanus

Lobsters are most active at night, but you might find one during the day hiding in a rock crevice. In winter, lobsters head for deeper water.

Look at the two large front claws. One has sharp inner points for holding and tearing prey, such as fish, clams, crabs, starfish, and other lobsters. The other claw has blunt edges for crushing and cracking shells and bones. The lobster uses its eight other much smaller legs for walking, swimming, and feeding. When a leg or claw breaks off, another can grow in its place. Sensors for taste and smell are located on the long antennae and over the whole shell.

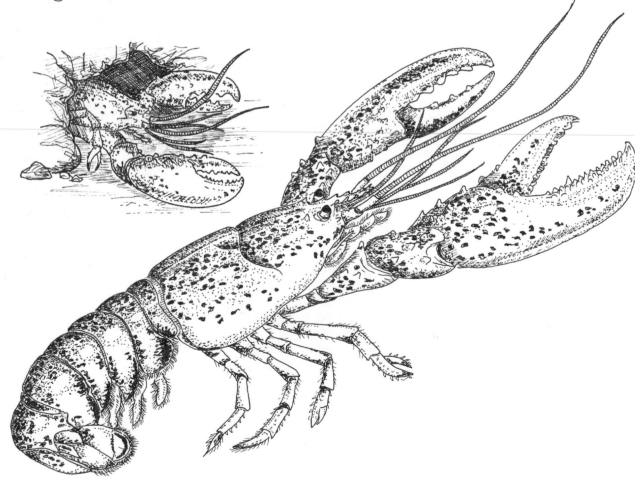

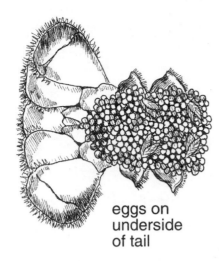
eggs on
underside
of tail

It takes a lobster about five years to grow to an edible size of about 1½ to 2 pounds. Some very old lobsters reach 40 to 50 pounds. The lobster's hard shell is called an exoskeleton. As a lobster grows larger, it sheds, or molts, its exoskeleton, many times.

Each year in June or July, the female lays about 15,000 eggs that cling to hairs under her tail until they hatch ten or eleven months later. As the larvae float around—eating, growing quickly, and shedding their skin—larger animals gobble them up. Of the 15,000 young, only about a dozen survive to become adults.

Lobstermen catch lobsters in boxlike wooden traps. The lobsters enter to eat the bait and cannot find their way out. Lobsters are unfriendly to each other and are always ready to fight, so they are difficult to raise on fish farms.

ROCK CRAB

Cancer irroratus

One of many types of crabs that scurry along the shore, the rock crab is yellowish with red or purplish brown speckles. It lives in shallow water on sandy, rocky, or gravel bottoms. You can count nine marginal teeth along the shell edge on each side of its eyes and three between the eyes.

It scurries around on its hind four pairs of legs looking for small marine animals, alive or dead, to eat. The enlarged front pair of legs are claws that can grab and tear apart prey. As the crab grows, its outside shell, or carapace, becomes too tight. Blood in the claws flows into the body, and the body shrinks a little. A slit forms across the back of the shell, and the crab backs out of its old shell, already wearing its new, soft shell. Before the new shell hardens, the animal is called a soft-shell crab. Many different species of crab go through this soft-shell stage.

FIDDLER CRAB

Uca pugilator

Fiddler crabs are easily identified by the male's greatly enlarged right or left front claw. He carries it like a fiddle and uses it in his dancelike courtship to attract a female. The male bows up and down, waves his claw, and rises on "tiptoe." The male uses his small claw, not the large claw, and the female uses both small claws to feed on algae, fungi, decayed grass, and bacteria. Sometimes they roll food up in small mud pellets before they eat it.

Fiddler crabs live in colonies in mudflats, marshes, and beaches, digging burrows 2 to 3 feet long. When the tide comes in, the crabs run into the burrow and close a trap door behind them. During winter they stay in a hibernation-like state inside the burrow.

HERMIT CRAB

Long-Clawed Hermit Crab *Pagurus longicarpus*

Unlike other crabs, the hind end of the hermit crab is soft, so they protect themselves by using abandoned shells as homes. As the crab grows, it replaces the old shell with a new, larger one. Two pairs of legs on the curved abdomen are adapted

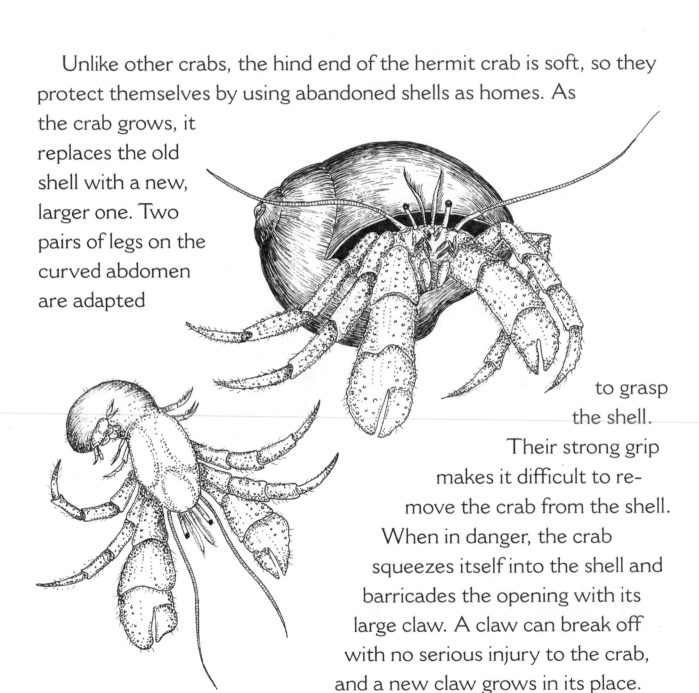

to grasp the shell. Their strong grip makes it difficult to remove the crab from the shell. When in danger, the crab squeezes itself into the shell and barricades the opening with its large claw. A claw can break off with no serious injury to the crab, and a new claw grows in its place.

MOLE CRAB

Emerita talpoida

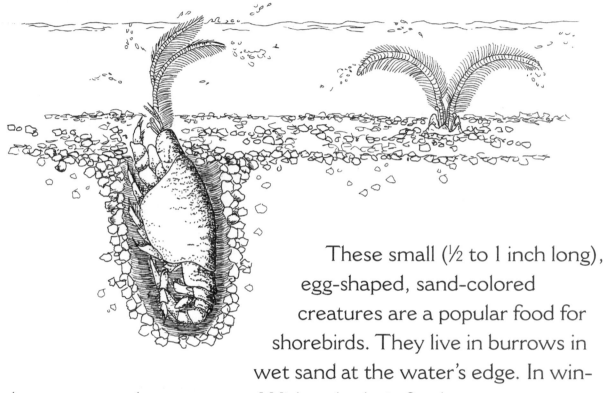

These small (½ to 1 inch long), egg-shaped, sand-colored creatures are a popular food for shorebirds. They live in burrows in wet sand at the water's edge. In winter, they move to deeper water. With only their feathery antennae sticking out of the burrow, they sweep organic matter into their mouths. Some people call them sand bugs, but they are really crabs. Don't worry—they don't bite.

You might confuse mole crabs with sand hoppers. The hopper is a bit larger (1 inch), and you will usually see it jumping at the water's edge. The mole crab spends most of its time almost submerged in wet sand. To find a mole crab, look for the feathery antennae projecting from the wet sand and dig with your hands or a small sand shovel.

HORSESHOE CRAB

Limulus polyphemus

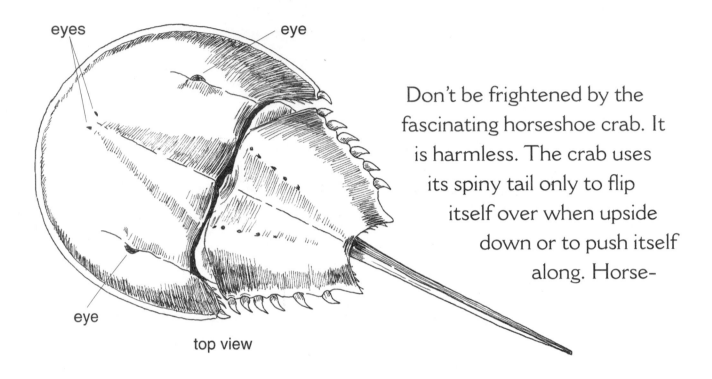

eyes

eye

eye

top view

Don't be frightened by the fascinating horseshoe crab. It is harmless. The crab uses its spiny tail only to flip itself over when upside down or to push itself along. Horse-

shoe crabs are not true crabs but are more closely related to spiders. They were alive millions of years ago—even before dinosaurs—and have barely changed, so they carry the nickname "living fossils."

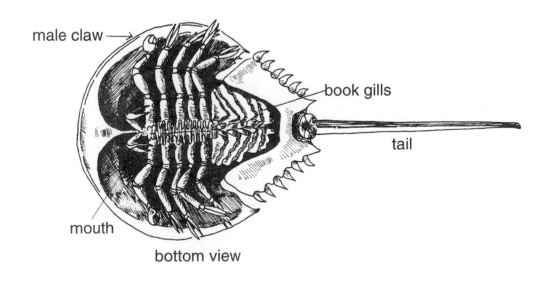

male claw

book gills

tail

mouth

bottom view

They have ten eyes, none as developed as our eyes. There are two large eyes on top and two smaller ones on the top front. Six smaller eyes are underneath near the mouth and on the tail, but they are hard to find. Horseshoe crabs cannot see objects but can detect light and dark.

The gills take oxygen from the water and, by flapping, help propel the crabs along. Because they look like the pages of a book, they are called book gills.

During spring high tides in the mating season, the smaller male grips the back of the larger female with special hooklike claws. She tows him into shore, digs a nest, and lays hundreds of greenish eggs. The male covers the eggs with sperm and conceals them with sand. In about two weeks, tiny young hatch from the eggs that have not been eaten by predators. These sand-colored babies try to hide in the sand until they are older. As they grow, they molt their shells many times for a new larger one. You may find these tiny shells washed up on shore. They look like dead crabs but are just shed shells.

The horseshoe crab's blood is milky white in water but turns blue in air because of copper in the blood, which helps carry oxygen. Horseshoe crab blood is used in medical research.

BARNACLE

Northern Rock Barnacle   *Balanus balanoides*

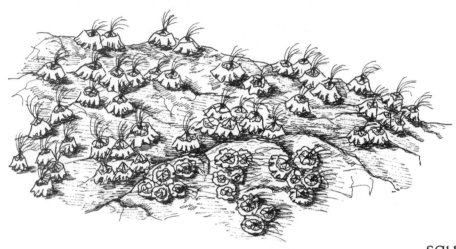

Barnacles are shrimplike animals that live in limy-plated, cone-shaped houses. The animals turn upside down and, by squeezing a powerful glue from their heads, attach to a spot for life. Their hard shells cover rocks and pilings in great numbers and with a grip so strong that they cannot be removed without breaking them. The few free-swimming larvae that hatch from eggs and escape being eaten settle on rocks, pilings, boat hulls, shells, or even on whales. Boats sometimes have to have the barnacles scraped off because they slow the boats down.

The six pairs of legs act as feathery appendages that stick out of the top and sweep microscopic plants and animals into the barnacle's mouth. When the tide goes out, moveable top plates close tightly, trapping a little water inside. The barnacle hides inside until the tide comes back, bringing more water and food.

larvae

adult

SAND HOPPER

Talorchestia megalophthalma

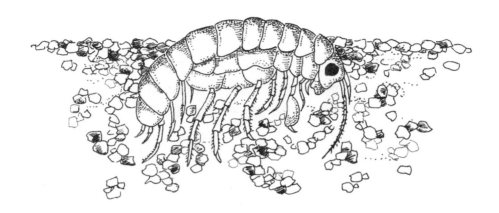

Have you ever picked up clumps of seaweed on the beach and disturbed large numbers of "beach fleas"? They are actually harmless crustaceans, not fleas (which are insects). By straightening their bent bodies, they can jump up to 72 times their own height. Sand hoppers are about 1 inch long, sand colored, and have narrow bodies. They must keep their gills moist, so they hide under debris or burrow in wet sand to avoid the hot sun. If submerged in water for long, they will drown.

FISH

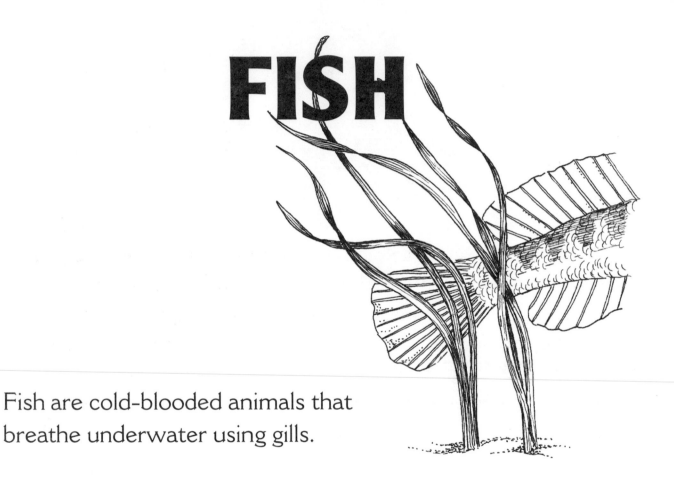

Fish are cold-blooded animals that breathe underwater using gills.

FLOUNDER

Pseudopleuronectes americanus

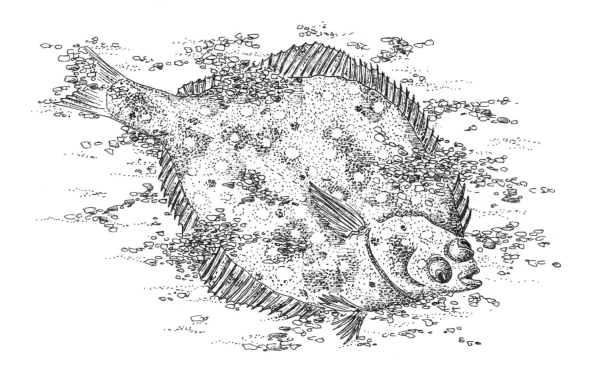

You might not see one of these flat fish until you step on it in shallow water. Experts at camouflage, their underside is pale but the top can match the color of pebbles, sand, mud, or even take on a checkerboard pattern. Pigment cells expand or contract to change patterns.

Amazingly, flounder start out like most other fish with an eye on each side. Slowly the left eye moves to the right side and the mouth twists upward a bit. The fish turns so the right side is up, and the lower side loses pigment. Now it swims flat along the bottom, eating food in the sand but able to watch for enemies above.

young

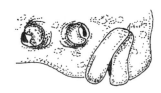

adult

MERMAID'S PURSE

Common Skate *Raja erinacea*

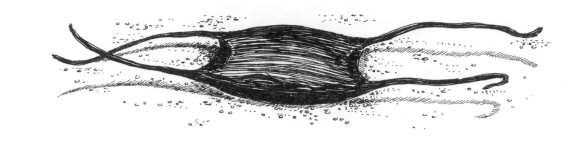

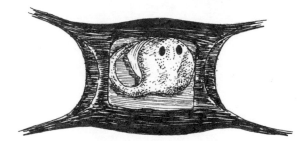

baby skate inside

These 4-to-6-inch-long leathery objects often wash up on the shore. They are skate egg cases that are deposited on the sandy or muddy bottom in shallow water. Curling tendrils at each corner anchor the cases to grass, wood, or rocks on the bottom while one or two baby skates grow inside. Skates have enlarged fins that look like wings on each side of their bodies. They swim with gentle wavelike movements of these wings. The head, body, and fins are flat. With their mouths on the bottom and eyes on top, skates swim close to the bottom, searching for crustaceans, shellfish, and fish to eat but keeping watch for attackers above.

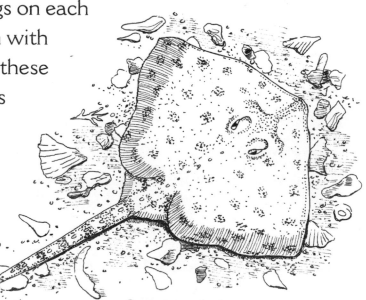

Common skate

SAND SHARK

Mustelus canis

This small, harmless shark rarely grows more than 3 feet long. Sand sharks hunt singly (usually) for plants and animals, especially their favorite food, crustaceans. The sand shark's sense of smell is well developed. As they swim, they swing their head from side to side scenting for their prey. Once they locate prey, they swim a figure eight around it and then attack.

Sand sharks give birth in the summer to four to twelve young, each about 1 foot long. They are sandy brown or gray.

SEA ROBIN

Prionotus evolans

You will never forget this fish because it looks so odd! Sea robins can reach 1½ feet long. The head has bony plates with the eyes placed high on the head. The pectoral fins are so large they look like wings—the source of the common name. Underneath, the two to three pectoral rays are enlarged and separate. The rays help them walk along the bottom, and scientists think they may also be sensitive to touch. Sea robins come in shades of gray or brown with some black bars or spots on the rays. Mollusks and crustaceans are the sea robin's main food. Watch for these fish resting on the sandy bottom and using their rays like fingers to explore the sand.

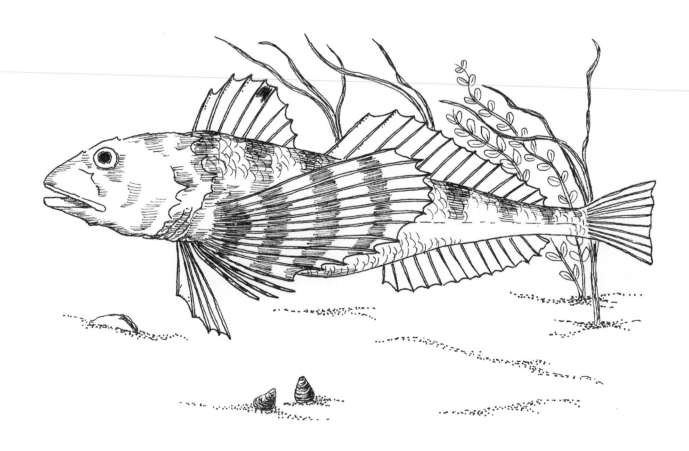

STRIPED BLENNY

Chasmodes bosquianus

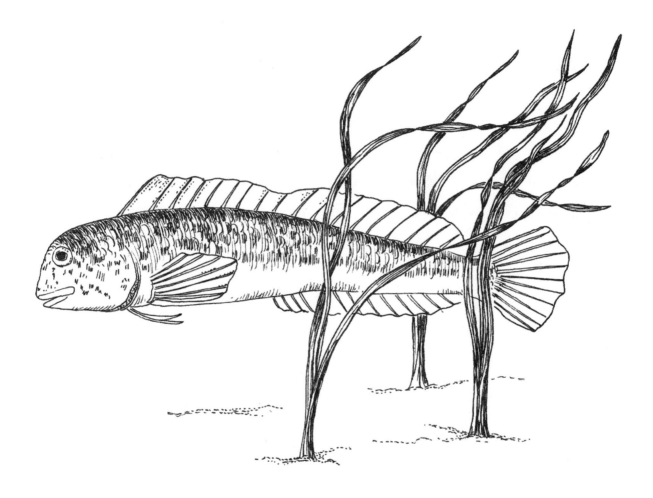

The striped blenny is a common fish in shallow water. They grow up to 5 inches long and are mottled yellow browns and grays, often with subtle stripes on the sides. The young are difficult to spot as they hide among weeds. Small mollusks and crustaceans are the striped blenny's favorite food. The fish's eggs are heavy and sticky, which helps them cling to empty shells and in crevices.

BUTTERFISH

Pholis gunellus

The butterfish's name comes from the slippery, slimy coating on its body. This helps it slide into small, rocky holes and crevices where it looks for worms, mollusks, and crustaceans to eat. Butterfish are long and narrow, up to 12 inches long, and come in various shades of brown and olive, sometimes even red. Though it looks like an eel, it is not. The common "true" eel is up to 5 feet long with tiny embedded scales, and with the top (dorsal) fin, tail fin, and anal (bottom) fin joined in one long, continuous fin.

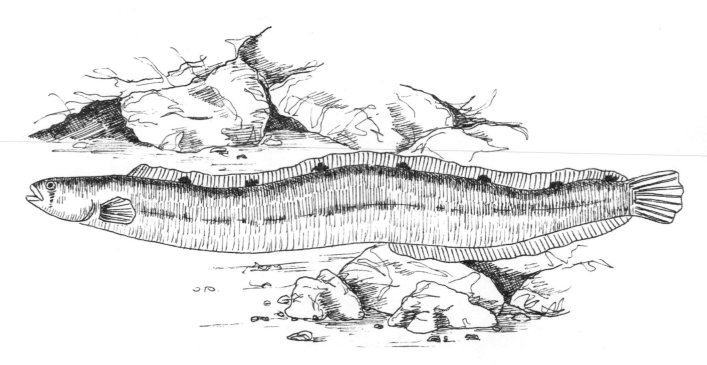

The butterfish lays its heavy, sticky eggs during the cooler months. The weight and stickiness allows them to stay in empty shells and crevices. The female fish sometimes curls around the eggs during incubation. Look for butterfish in tide pools and rock crevices.

NAKED GOBY

Gobiosoma bosci

This small fish (up to 2 inches long) is commonly found in grassy bays and tide pools. Their mottled light and dark brown coloring makes them difficult to spot among shells, grasses, and shadows. Small crustaceans are their favorite food. Notice that the naked goby's eyes are close to the top of its head. Many inshore fish have eye placement like this so they can watch for predators, such as birds, from above.

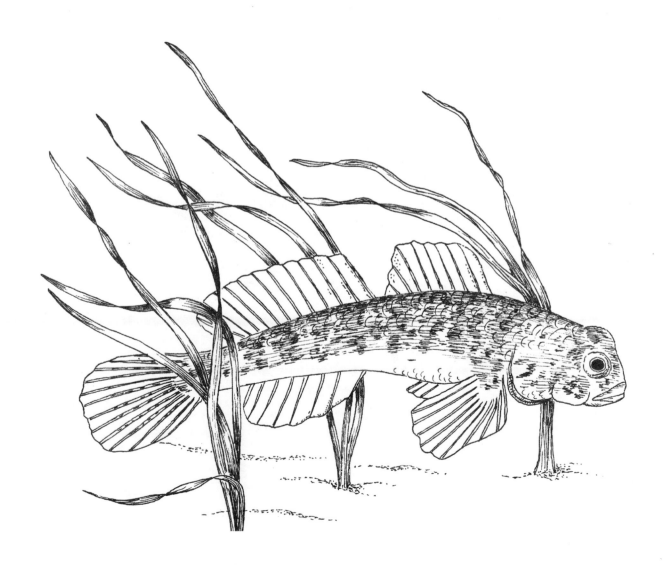

CUNNER

Tautogolabrus adspersus

You will find these fish around wharves and where the bottom is rocky. They eat almost anything—seaweed, microscopic creatures, crustaceans, mollusks, and fish. They can crush mollusks easily with their powerful teeth. Cunners grow 12 to 15 inches long and can weigh 2½ pounds.

Cunners lay their eggs in June and July. Being buoyant and nonadhesive, the eggs drift in the sea. At water temperatures around 72° F, they hatch in about forty hours. Most other members of this family are tropical fish.

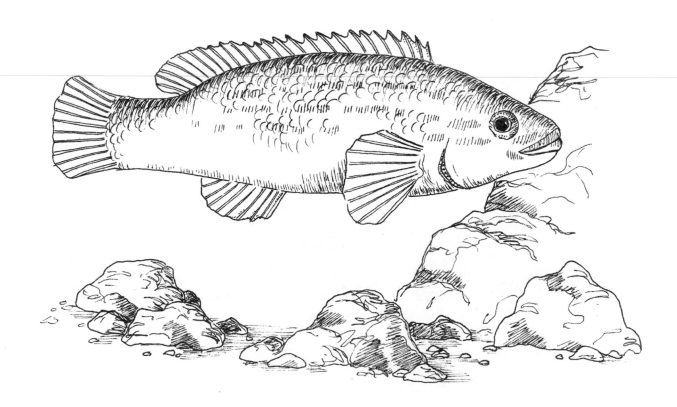

SEA TURTLE

Large turtles adapted
for a life of swimming, sea
turtles are rarely seen on land.

GREEN SEA TURTLE

Chelonia mydas

The green sea turtle's limbs are well adapted to swimming. The animals rarely come to land except at night during the breeding season, from March to May. The female lays about 100 eggs in a hole on a sandy beach, above the high tide line so they are not washed away. About 45 to 50 days later, the babies hatch and struggle to reach the ocean without being eaten by such predators as birds and small mammals. Green sea turtles, plant eaters themselves, grow to 4 feet long and weigh 300 to 400 pounds. This animal's name comes from internal green fat deposits. Its outer shell and flippers are usually in shades of brown.

Occasionally, a dead adult washes ashore. Numbers of green sea turtles have decreased because of pollution, loss of nest sites, egg collectors, being harvested as food, and dying in nets. Also the green sea turtle is the turtle most sought after by humans for food.

Look for four plates in the shell between the top and the margin.

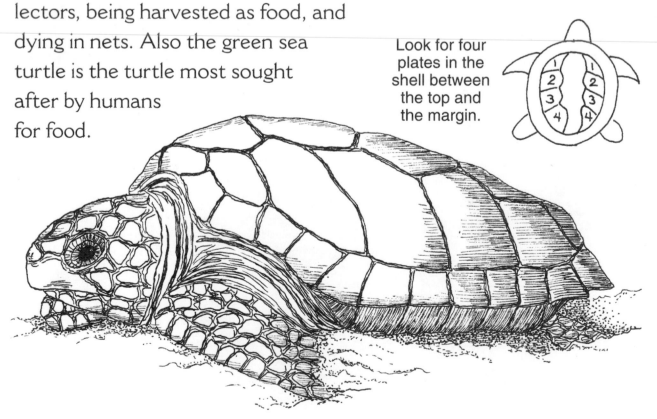

SEA MAMMALS

These animals are warm-blooded, bear live young, produce milk for their young, and grow hair. Watch for sea mammals offshore while you are beachcombing.

HUMPBACK WHALE

Megaptera novaeangliae

If you are lucky you might experience the
thrill of spotting a humpback whale offshore.
Like many whales, humpbacks were hunted
almost to extinction. Now, with protection,
they are making a
comeback.

The humpback whale weighs up to 40 tons and is about the size of a freight-train car. It has long winglike flippers and knobs on its head. Individual whales can be identified by the color patterns of their tails.

Humpbacks are known for a typical behavior called breaching. They leap high in the air then fall sideways or backwards with a big splash. Scientists think whales breach for fun or to shake off pests.

As mammals, whales breathe oxygen. They exhale their breath as spouts through nostrils on top of the head. From shore, you might see a whale's exhaled spouts before you see the animal itself. Each species has a distinctive spout shape.

humpback   sperm   blue   right

Instead of teeth, humpbacks have baleen, giant brushes made from horny plates. The whale gulps large amounts of water then forces it

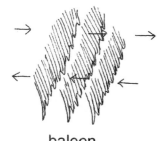

baleen

out through the baleen. The fringed edges of baleen trap the plankton and small fish that the whale eats.

Humpbacks utter hauntingly beautiful songs. The males sing to attract females, and the song carries over long distances—up to 115 miles.

PILOT WHALE

Globicephala melas

Pilot whales are relatively small, averaging 15 to 20 feet long. They are black with a light patch on the chest and along the midline and have a very round head. Their favorite food is squid.

No other whale is stranded on beaches as often and in such large numbers as the pilot whale. Scientists do not know why whales become stranded, but they have many theories. Inner ear infections may upset balance or echolocation. Whales use echolocation to navigate and hunt, sending out a sound and waiting for the sound to bounce back, or echo, to their ears. Then they can locate the object that the sound bounced off. The whales may become disoriented in shallow or unfamiliar waters. Magnetic disturbances or stormy weather may hinder them. Pilot whales travel in schools, and when a leader heads into shore, others typically follow.

DOLPHIN

Atlantic Bottlenosed Dolphin *Tursiops truncatus*

The most common dolphin on the Atlantic coast, the bottlenosed is also the one you will most likely see performing in captivity. These intelligent, soft gray mammals can grow up to

12 feet long. A transverse groove that separates the short beak from the forehead makes them look like they are always smiling. Bottlenosed dolphins click, whistle, and chirp to communicate with other dolphins. To help locate and capture fish, they send out ultrasonic signals that bounce back, telling them the location of their prey. This is called echolocation.

The number of bottlenosed dolphins has decreased in recent years because of pollution and drowning in fishnets.

HARBOR SEAL

Phoca vitulina

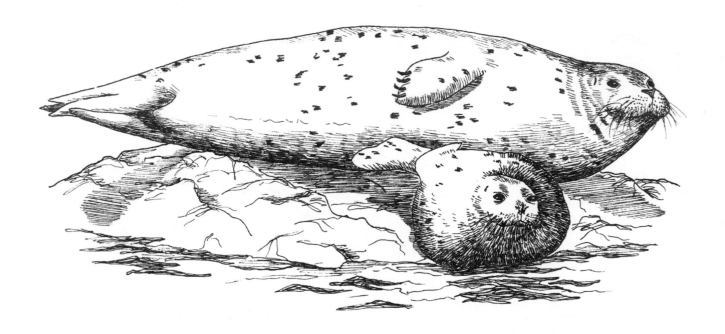

You might see this doglike seal peeking out of the water or basking on some rocks. Their color varies from brown to gray, often with dark or light spots. They are of little value for fur, hides, or oil—but they are fun to watch. Harbor seals have no outer ear, just a small hole or opening in the skin. Their flippers do not turn forward, so they have to wiggle their whole body to move on land. Compared with other seals, they spend a lot of time on land.

Harbor seals mate in the water or on land. The young are born in early spring, when the animals gather in small herds on sandbars, ledges, and islands. Harbor seals eat squid, shellfish, and fish. They can stay underwater up to half an hour and can dive 300 feet deep.

Harbor seals are true seals because they lack ear flaps and cannot turn their hind limbs forward. Sea lions, which are often mistaken for seals, have ear flaps and can turn their hind limbs forward.

BIRDS

Birds are warm-blooded animals known for their unique ability to fly and their distinctive feathers. Many shorebirds acquire colorful plumage in spring to attract mates. By fall, their coloration turns to the more drab winter plumage.

DOUBLE-CRESTED CORMORANT

Phalacrocorax auritus

On rocks offshore, you may see glossy black, goose-size birds with their wings outspread and their necks bent in an **S**. These are double-crested cormorants. The cormorant's feathers lack oil for waterproofing, enabling the bird to swim underwater easily to catch fish. However, that means that when cormorants swim, their plumage gets wet. You may see the birds on rocks or in trees with their wings spread to dry. The cormorant's bill is hooked at the tip, with an orange pouch underneath. Both sexes sport a crest on both sides of their heads. The crests disappear during nesting and may be hard to see if the bird is far away.

Cormorants nest in trees or on rocky ledges. The nest of sticks, seaweed, and grass can form a platform 3 feet high and 2 feet across. The female lays three to four blue eggs. By the time the young are ten weeks old, they can dive and fly and are completely independent.

COMMON TERN

Sterna hirundo

Terns are small (13 to 16 inches long), graceful birds. Superb fliers, they can hover, flit, and dive into the water to capture fish and shrimp. Their small, weak feet are not useful for much walking or swimming. Common terns have black caps, orange bills with black tips, and pale gray backs and wings. In winter, their bills are all black, and the black caps are incomplete, covering just the back of the head and under the eye. Take a moment to watch these fantastic flyers.

During the mating season, the male presents a small fish to a female. They pass it back and forth, and if she finally eats it, she has chosen that male as her mate. The nest is a hollow in the sand, maybe with a little grass lining it. Once the three brown-spotted buff eggs hatch, both parents tend the young.

HERRING GULL

Larus argentatus

Although commonly called "seagulls," most gulls do not live far out at sea. They do fly far inland, however, following rivers, lakes, and coastlines. They eat a variety of foods—fruit, eggs, nestlings, marine animals, garbage, and carrion—and so can live in many habitats. The herring gull has pink legs and feet, a gray back, white-spotted black wing tips, and a red spot on its yellow beak. When young peck at the spot, parents regurgitate food for the young to eat. The mottled brown plumage of immature gulls gradually whitens over several years as they get older.

Gulls nest on the ground, typically in the dunes, making crude nests of seaweed, trash, and sticks. Adults may eat other gulls' chicks. Of every five eggs laid, only one chick lives to fly. Young are independent when six weeks old.

RED KNOT

Calidris canutus

Watch for these medium-size shorebirds as they fly, turn, and dip in unison in large flocks. You will see the brown on their backs alternating with their red bellies in spring plumage. In fall, the red knot's plumage becomes gray on the back with white underparts. Large flocks comb the shores, drilling the sand with their bills for mollusks and crustaceans. Knots commonly stand on one foot with their beak tucked against one side.

Red knots breed in the Arctic tundra. Their nest is a small depression in the ground or on rock, lined with lichens. They lay four brown-spotted, olive buff eggs. Knots make a 20,000-mile round-trip between the Arctic and Antarctic Oceans every year. During their migration, you may spot their flocks along the Atlantic coast.

SEMIPALMATED PLOVER

Charadrius semipalmatus

You can easily identify these common birds by the one dark band across the chest and the dark back. Semipalmated plovers are plump and 6 to 8 inches long, with brown backs, orange yellow legs, partly webbed feet, and yellow beaks with black tips. In winter, the black band across the chest turns brown, and the entire bill turns black. These birds run behind a receding wave and stab at the sand as they look for crustaceans, mollusks, worms, and insects. Plovers often run along the beach, stop short, raise their heads, then run again.

Semipalmated plovers breed in the far north. The nest is a shallow depression in the ground lined with small pebbles, shell pieces, or bits of vegetation. They lay four brown-spotted buff eggs. These plovers visit our region as they migrate between the north country and their winter home in California or the Gulf Coast.

BLACK-BELLIED PLOVER

Pluvialis squatarola

In breeding plumage, these pretty plovers have black breasts, faces, and bills, with pale speckled backs. The forehead, nape, crown, and sides of the breast are white. Their coloring is unusual—most other birds are dark above and pale below. In winter, the plumage becomes pale and speckled underneath. Black-bellied plovers are stocky, 10 to 13 inches long, and fast runners. Running and stabbing the sand on tidal flats, sandbars, and marshes, they capture worms, mollusks, and crustaceans. They usually travel in small groups or singly, not in large flocks.

The black-bellied plover's nest is a shallow depression, lined with grass or lichens, in the ground or in the moss of the tundra. The four black-spotted eggs vary from buff or gray to pink or even greenish.

LEAST SANDPIPER

Calidris minutilla

Nicknamed "peeps," least sandpipers are one of the smallest (sparrow-size) shorebirds. Sometimes they are so unwary that you almost step on them before they fly up in unison, wheel overhead, and settle back on the sand. Least sandpipers prefer grassy areas in marshes and along shores. With sensitive beaks they probe for tiny mole crabs and other food. Look for yellow green legs, streaked breasts, and brownish backs.

Least sandpipers breed in the far north, nesting in a small, grass- or moss-lined depression in the tundra. They normally lay four brown-spotted, pinkish buff eggs.

SPOTTED SANDPIPER

Actitis macularia

Spotted sandpipers are fun to watch as they teeter and bob their rear ends up and down—all the while looking for small fish, insects, and crustaceans along the shore. These robin-size (7 to 8 inches) birds have beautiful round breast spots in summer, but by fall and winter the spots disappear. Spotted sandpipers have olive brown backs and a white line over each eye. When flushed, they fly with a few fast wingbeats followed by a short glide.

Many of our shorebirds breed in the far north, but this one nests in much of the United States and Canada. The nest is a depression in the ground lined with moss or grass. The female lays four buff eggs with brown spots.

SANDERLING

Calidris alba

You may have seen these small shorebirds as they run in front of an incoming wave and then chase the wave as it recedes. They are searching for tiny crustaceans and mollusks at the water's edge. Sanderlings are about the size of a starling (7 to 8 inches), with black bills and legs and distinct white wing stripes. In summer, the backs, heads, and chests are rusty brown, contrasting with the white belly. In winter, they become pale gray above, with black shoulders and white bellies.

Sanderlings breed along the coasts of the Arctic Ocean. They lay four brown-spotted olive eggs in a depression in the ground lined with lichens and grass. These shorebirds migrate far into the Southern Hemisphere and are found on almost every beach in the world.

RUDDY TURNSTONE

Arenaria interpres

As the name implies, these birds look for food by turning over stones—as well as shells, driftwood, seaweed, mud, and other debris—with their bills. They also dig deep holes in search of burrowing crustaceans. Sometimes these holes are as big as the birds (8 to 10 inches.) In their colorful spring plumage, they are reddish brown above and white below, with black-and-white patterns on their heads and chests and orange legs. Their winter plumage is much duller, although the bib pattern and orange leg color remain.

Another Arctic breeder, the turnstone nests in a grass-lined depression in the tundra or in the dunes. They lay four spotted, buff olive eggs, which the pugnacious adults defend against any intruders, including humans.

GREAT BLUE HERON

Ardea herodias

One of the largest birds in North America (up to 4 feet), this heron has a soft blue gray body, white around the head, and black head patch and plumes. Great blue herons are fascinating to watch as they stalk prey in slow motion or stand motionless for a half hour before suddenly striking at prey. The sharp bill can spear food or be used as scissors. Great blue herons can lift a foot without rippling the water. Their food includes fish, snakes, frogs, birds, small mammals, and insects.

Great blue herons nest in colonies, their droppings typically washing the branches below in white. They build stick nests high in treetops or sometimes in low shrubs or on the ground. They lay three to five greenish blue eggs.

ATLANTIC PUFFIN

Fratercula arctica

If you are lucky, you might spot these odd birds on rocky cliffs along the shore. Their upright stance and colorful markings make them look like clowns. The stubby Atlantic puffin is black above and white below, with gray cheeks and orange feet. The flat and triangular bill has a slate gray base, red tip, and yellow trim during the breeding season. After mating season, the colorful plates fall off the bill, and it becomes brownish with some yellow. Juveniles have much smaller and less colorful bills, developing the full adult bill over their first five years.

Marvelous swimmers, puffins look like they fly underwater after small fish, their favorite prey. Puffins swallow fish underwater, unless they are bringing some back to feed their young. One egg is laid in a grass-lined burrow in a rock crevice or soft soil. After six weeks' care, the young are left to fend for themselves.

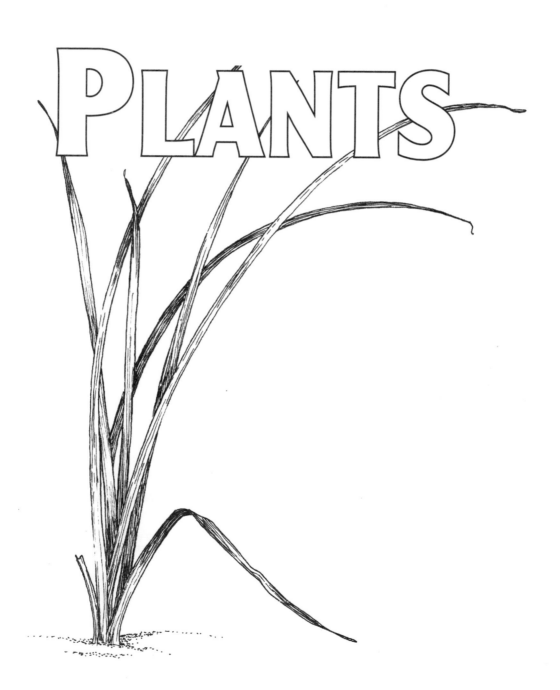

PLANTS

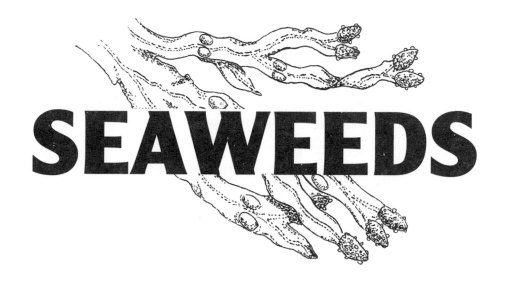

SEAWEEDS

Seaweeds lack true leaves, flowers, roots, or stems. The leaf-like fronds photosynthesize and produce a jellylike coating that prevents water loss in the sun and wind. Seeds, which normally are produced in flowers, are not needed because seaweeds release reproductive cells directly into the water. A holdfast that looks like a root anchors the plant to sand or rock. The holdfast does not absorb nutrients as roots do because the plant is bathed in nutrient-rich water. Stems are not needed because the plants can float in water.

Seaweeds with red pigment can photosynthesize in the deepest water with the least light. Those with brown pigment photosynthesize at medium depths of up to 75 feet. Those with green pigment live in shallow water with the greatest light.

IRISH MOSS

Chondrus crispus

Look for clumps of Irish moss on the beach or floating in the shallows. This purplish red or purplish green seaweed has flattened blades that divide into many forked ends. Irish moss produces a gelatin that is used as a thickener in soups and dairy products, and in shoe polish, soap, and cosmetics. It is gathered commercially on some maritime beaches.

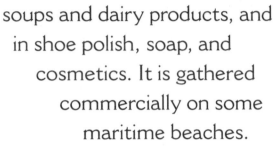

DULSE

Palmaria palmata

This seaweed has large rosy red blades that feel rubbery. Some people eat it as a vegetable or add it to soup. It can even be dried and eaten raw—though this takes getting used to. In some places people harvest it commercially, drying it, bagging it, and selling it in stores.

Like most red seaweeds, the red pigment can photosynthesize well in dim underwater light, so it grows at greater depths than green seaweeds. Small fish, crabs, mollusks, and other creatures hide among or hold onto the dulse's waving blades.

BLADDER WRACK

Fucus vesiculosus

At some time most beach-combers have popped the air bladders of bladder wrack they find on the beaches. In rough water these bladders help keep the leathery brown fronds afloat. The bumpy sacs at the end of the blades hold male and female cells that are released into the water for fertilization. Bladder wrack, a member of the rockweed family, is one of the most widely distributed seaweeds. It covers rocks and wood pilings in large mats, providing shelter for many small animals.

KELP

Sugar Kelp *Laminaria saccharina*

This brown seaweed has a long (up to 10 feet), ruffled, leathery blade that floats with currents. The rootlike hold-fast anchors it firmly to rocks. Mats of kelp form an ideal habitat for many marine creatures, such as sea urchins, starfish, periwinkles, crabs, and small fish, which either attach to the blades or swim under the mat's cover. A sweet-tasting powder forms on the blades as they dry out, giving this species its common name and its species name.

SEA LETTUCE

Ulva lactuca

Sea lettuce is easily identified because it looks so much like salad lettuce—but it does not taste particularly good to humans. Light green, tissue-thin sheets are about 12 inches long. Sea lettuce attaches to rocks or wood or floats in shallow water. It tolerates fresh water or mild pollution for a time.

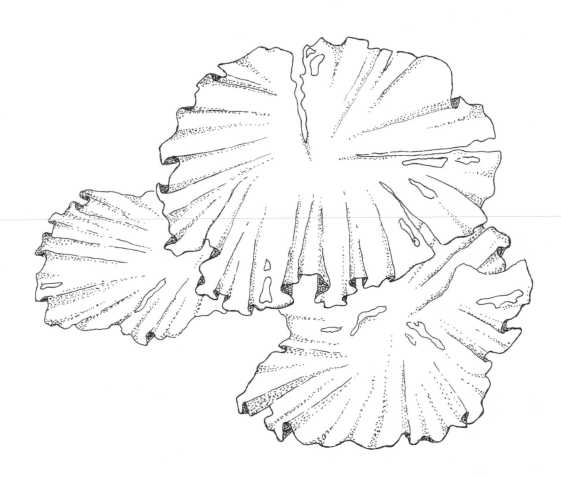

FLOWERING PLANTS

Beach plants have true leaves, flowers, roots, and stems. They have small leaves that are waxy, leathery, or hairy, which helps them retain moisture and resist drying from wind, sun, or salt spray. Some roots grow very deep into sand and cliffs searching for water. Extensive root systems are helpful in anchoring the plant in sand. Underground stems, called rhizomes, make it easier for new shoots to develop instead of waiting for seeds to germinate.

DUSTY MILLER

Artemisia stelleriana

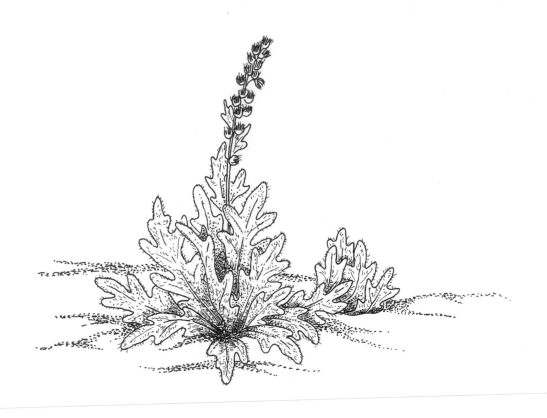

This perennial herb from Asia has colonized our eastern beaches. You can recognize dusty miller by the pale green leaves covered with fuzzy hairs, which reduce evaporation from the leaves. Small yellow flowers bloom from July to September. This hardy plant grows up to 24 inches tall and inhabits dune areas nearest the sea. Dusty miller is closely related to the sagebrush of our western deserts.

BEACH PEA

Lathyrus japonicus

This pretty, trailing vine has lavender pealike flowers that bloom through the summer. Long curly tendrils cling to other plants as the beach pea spreads along the ground, anchoring it against strong winds and blowing sand.
Long narrow seedpods form after blooming. The hardy beach pea grows in dune areas nearest the sea.

BEACH HEATH

Hudsonia tomentosa

Beach heath grows low to the ground in mats. The tiny scalelike leaves are gray and woolly. By growing close to the stem, the leaves are less likely to dry out. Small yellow flowers open only in the sun and last just one day, blooming sometime between May and July.

Beach heath is also known as poverty grass because it can grow in nutrient-poor sandy soil. The stems tend to form mats, which help to slow erosion in the dunes.

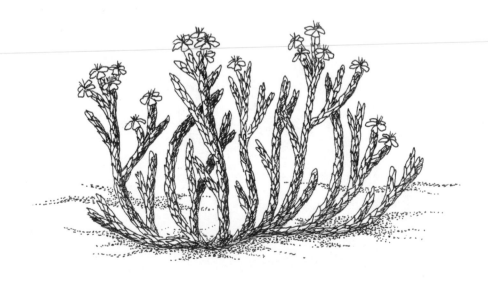

SEA ROCKET

Cakile edentula

    Sea rocket is easy to recognize by its rocket-shaped seed capsules.
They form after pale lavender flowers bloom in July to September.
The stems and leaves are very fleshy and thick, which enables them to
store water easily. Sea rocket belongs to the mustard family, and its
young stems and leaves have a biting horseradish-like flavor. Look for
these plants above the high-tide line.

BAYBERRY

Northern Bayberry *Myrica pensylvanica*

Early settlers knew bayberry well as a source of wax for candles. The stems are covered with clusters of gray waxy berries. When the fruit are put in boiling water, the wax rises to the surface. It takes several bushels of berries, however, to make one candle. The leathery leaves can be used in cooking and give off a spicy aroma when crushed. Northern bayberry grows as a low, sprawling shrub in protected areas of dunes.

EELGRASS

Zostera marina

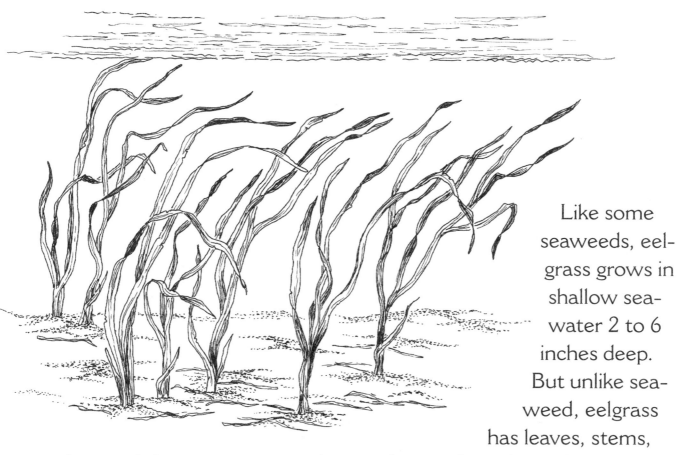

Like some seaweeds, eelgrass grows in shallow seawater 2 to 6 inches deep. But unlike seaweed, eelgrass has leaves, stems, and roots. It is not a true grass but a relative of pond weeds. Eelgrass spreads along creeping underground stems, or rhizomes, and also by seeds. Very small male and female flowers are hidden in the leaf sheaths. Male flowers produce gelatinous pollen that they release into the water. When the pollen finds a female flower, fertilization occurs and seeds are produced.

Eelgrass plays several important roles in its environment. The grass grows in dense mats that soften wave action. The roots stabilize bottom sediment. Many creatures, including worms, snails, algae, crabs, lobsters, sponges, fish, and clams, live among its leaves. When the plants die back in autumn, the dead leaves drop and increase organic matter in the water. Eelgrass is also a valuable food for ducks and geese.

BEACH GRASS

Ammophila breviligulata

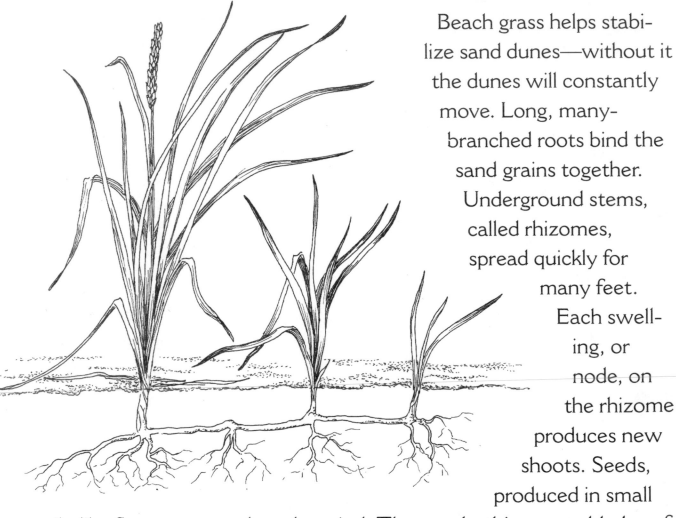

Beach grass helps stabilize sand dunes—without it the dunes will constantly move. Long, many-branched roots bind the sand grains together. Underground stems, called rhizomes, spread quickly for many feet. Each swelling, or node, on the rhizome produces new shoots. Seeds, produced in small spikelike flowers, spread on the wind. The tough, thin, green blades of grass, up to 2 feet tall, roll up to conserve moisture on hot days and unroll to catch moisture.

This hardy plant grows on sandy dunes close to the sea. Beach grass thrives in sand, needing the sand to stimulate root production. Sand dropped by wind at the plant's base insulates it from heat. Beach grass tolerates cold winters and flourishes in average daily temperatures of 70° to 80° F—any warmer and they cannot manufacture food.

CORDGRASS

Spartina patens

This low-growing, green grass (12 to 16 inches tall) is common in salt marshes. You can recognize it because the previous year's growth forms large flat mats, and the grass appears tousled and messy.

These dense mats prevent other types of plants from germinating in the immediate area. New cordgrass growth develops from shoots sent out from underground rhizomes as well as seeds.

Cordgrass has several adaptations that allow it to grow in salt water. The root membranes screen out much of the salt. Glands on the leaves can excrete salt. Any salt remaining inside the cells is concentrated so that it will not interfere with other cell processes.

SALT-MARSH BULRUSH

Scirpus robustus

Salt-marsh bulrush is especially valuable to animals of the salt marsh. The seeds are a favorite food of ducks and other marsh birds. The stems offer cover to many birds and animals, and they are eaten by raccoons, muskrats, and geese. Sedges, like this bulrush, play an important role as soil anchors and land builders in low-lying and flooded areas.

Upright green stems up to 6 feet tall grow singly or in groups and are triangular like all sedges. Red brown spikelets made of overlapping scales grow against the stem and contain tiny florets.

JOINTED GLASSWORT

Salicornia europaea

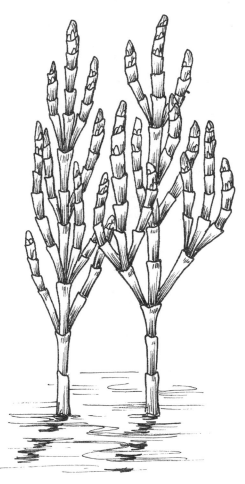

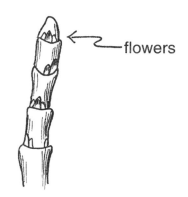

flowers

This striking annual grows in salt marshes, reaching a height of 6 to 18 inches. Its smooth, fleshy, branching stems can store large quantities of water for use when times are dry. If you pierce a piece of glasswort, you will see the moisture ooze out. Glasswort has the amazing ability to grow in soils and wet areas with high salt contents, places that would kill many other plants. Tiny flowers grow in threes in the upper joints. In fall, the stems turn a lovely red. Early settlers used to pickle the stems or add them raw to salads.

SEA LAVENDER

Limonium carolinianum

This pretty perennial is not related to the herb lavender. Small (⅛ inch) light purple or lavender pink flowers grow along one side of the stem. Sea lavender grows 8 to 20 inches tall and has spoon-shaped leaves. Dense colonies grow in some salt marshes, salt meadows, and dunes. An astringent mouthwash was once made from this plant's rootstock. Overpicking of sea lavender for bouquets has robbed many salt marshes of this plant's lovely purple cast. Please leave sea lavender where you find it, for all to enjoy.

Geographic Distribution of Plants and Animals Described in This Book

Barnacle *(Balanus balanoides):* On rocks and wood from the Arctic to Delaware.

Bayberry *(Myrica pensylvanica):* In swamps, sand, and woodlots from Nova Scotia and Newfoundland to North Carolina, and inland to Ohio.

Beach Heath *(Hudsonia tomentosa):* In sandy areas from New Brunswick to North Carolina, also the Great Lakes to Minnesota.

Beach Pea *(Lathyrus japonicus):* In sandy areas from Labrador to New Jersey, along the Great Lakes.

Bladder Wrack *(Fucus vesiculosus):* Common on rocky shores from the Arctic to the Carolinas.

Blenny, Striped *(Chasmodes bosquianus):* In shallow water from New York to Florida.

Boat Shell *(Crepidula fornicata):* On almost any hard objects in shallow water from the Gulf of St. Lawrence to Florida and Texas; introduced into central California.

Bulrush, Salt-Marsh *(Scirpus robustus):* In salt marshes from Massachusetts to Florida, west to Texas, the California coast to Mexico and South America.

Butterfish *(Pholis gunellus):* In tide pools and rock crevices from the Atlantic coast south to Massachusetts, rarely to New Jersey.

Clam, Razor *(Enis directus):* In sandy bottoms from Labrador to Florida.

Clam, Soft-Shell *(Mya arenaria):* In sand or mud bottoms in shallow water from Labrador to North Carolina; introduced into California and spread to Alaska.

Coral, Northern Stony *(Astrangia danae):* On rocks and shells in water to 120 feet deep, from Cape Cod to Florida.

Cordgrass *(Spartina patens):* Newfoundland and Quebec south along the coast to Texas, and inland in salt marshes.

Cormorant, Double-Crested *(Phalacrocorax auritus):* Along the coast anywhere the water is deep enough for fish; across most of North America, winters to British Hondurus.

Crab, Fiddler *(Uca pugilator):* In sand, mud, and marsh from Boston Harbor to Florida and Texas, and in the West Indies.

Crab, Horseshoe *(Limulus polyphemus):* On muddy or sandy bottoms from the Gulf of Maine to the Gulf of Mexico.

Crab, Hermit *(Pagurus longicarpus):* On rocky and sandy bottoms from Nova Scotia to Florida and Texas.

Crab, Mole *(Emerita talpoida):* At the water's edge from Labrador to South Carolina.

Crab, Rock *(Cancer irroratus):* On rocky and sandy bottoms from Labrador to South Carolina.

Cunner *(Tautogolabrus adspersus):* Common around wharves and on rocky bottoms from Labrador to New Jersey, rarely to Chesapeake Bay.

Dolphin, Atlantic Bottlenosed *(Tursiops truncatus):* Cape Cod to Florida.

Dulse *(Palmaria palmata):* Attached to rocks and shells from the Arctic to New Jersey.

Dusty Miller *(Artemisia stelleriana):* In sandy areas from the Gulf of St. Lawrence to Virginia, also around the Great Lakes.

Eelgrass *(Zostera marina):* Submerged in brackish water from the Arctic to South Carolina, the Pacific Coast.

Flounder *(Pseudopleuronectes americanus):* On sandy and muddy bottoms from Labrador to Georgia.

Glasswort, Jointed *(Salicornia europaea):* In salt marshes from New Brunswick and Nova Scotia to Georgia, locally in Michigan, Wisconsin, and Illinois.

Goby, Naked *(Gobiosoma bosci):* In shallows and grassy bays from Cape Cod to Florida.

Grass, Beach *(Ammophila breviligulata):* In sandy areas from Newfoundland to North Carolina, around the Great Lakes.

Gull, Herring *(Larus argentatus):* Along the coast and far inland along rivers in the northern parts of the Northern Hemisphere.

Heron, Great Blue *(Ardea herodias):* In lakes, rivers, and marshes on the coast and inland from southern Canada to the West Indies, Mexico; winters to South America.

Jellyfish, Moon *(Aurelia aurita):* In ocean waters at the whim of currents and waves from the Arctic to Florida and Mexico, Alaska to southern California.

Jingle Shell *(Anomia simplex):* On rocks and wood from Maine to Florida and Texas, the Bahamas, the West Indies.

Kelp, Sugar *(Laminaria saccharina):* Attached to rocks below the low-tide line from the Arctic to Massachusetts.

Knot, Red *(Calidris canutus):* Migrates along beaches and tidal flats and found in tundra in the Arctic; circumpolar, winters to the Southern Hemisphere.

Lavender, Sea *(Limonium carolinianum):* In salt marshes and dunes from Newfoundland and Quebec to Florida, west to Mississippi and Texas.

Limpet *(Notoacmaea testudinalis):* On rocks from the Arctic to Long Island Sound.

Lobster *(Homarus americanus):* On rocky and sandy bottoms from Labrador to Virginia.

Lugworm *(Arenicola cristata):* On sandy bottoms from Cape Cod to Florida and Louisiana, entire Pacific coast.

Mermaid's Purse: Egg case of skates that inhabit the coasts of North America.

Moon Shell *(Lunatia heros):* On sandy bottoms from Labrador to North Carolina.

Moss, Irish *(Chondrus crispus):* Labrador to Long Island Sound.

Mussel, Blue *(Mytilus edulis):* On rocks and wood from the Arctic to South Carolina, Alaska to Baja California.

Oyster *(Crassostrea virginica):* On rocks and wood from the Gulf of St. Lawrence to Florida and Texas, the Bahamas, the West Indies, introduced on the Pacific Coast.

Periwinkle *(Littorina littorea):* On rock, sand, and wood from Labrador to Maryland; also in central California.

Plover, Black-Bellied *(Pluvialis squatarola):* On tundra, beaches, coastal marshes, and less commonly at inland lakeshores in the Arctic; circumpolar; winters in the coastal United States and southern Eurasia to Southern Hemisphere.

Plover, Semipalmated *(Charadrius semipalmatus):* Along beaches, salt marshes, and lakeshores in the interior in Arctic America; winters in South America.

Portuguese Man-of-War *(Physalia physalia):* Drifts and is blown at sea and sometimes close to shore from Florida to Texas and Mexico, the Bahamas, the West Indies; driven as far north as Cape Cod in storms.

Puffin, Atlantic *(Fratercula arctica):* In rocky areas on the coast and islands of southern Greenland and Iceland to New England; also the British Isles.

Quahog, Northern *(Mercenaria mercenaria):* Burrows in sandy bottoms from the Gulf of St. Lawrence to Florida and Texas; introduced to California.

Sand Dollar *(Echinarachnius parma):* On sandy bottoms from Labrador to Maryland, Alaska to Puget Sound.

Sanderling *(Calidris alba):* Arctic circumpolar, winters from the United States, Britain, and China to the Southern Hemisphere.

Sand Hopper *(Talorchestia megalophthalma):* At the beach edge from Newfoundland to Florida.

Sandpiper, Least *(Calidris minutilla):* Common in grassy and muddy parts of marsh flats in Alaska and Canada; winters in southern United States to Brazil.

Sandpiper, Spotted *(Actitis macularia):* Almost anyplace with water nearby from Alaska and Canada to central United States, winters in southern United States to northern Argentina.

Scallop, Atlantic Bay *(Argopecten irradians):* On sandy and muddy bottoms from Cape Cod to Florida and Texas.

Sea Anemone, Northern Red *(Tealia felina):* On rocks and wood from the Arctic to Cape Cod, Alaska to central California.

Sea Cucumber, Orange-Footed *(Cucumaria frondosa):* On rocky and sandy bottoms from the Arctic to Cape Cod.

Sea Lettuce *(Ulva lactuca):* In shallow water, on rocks, and in mudflats from James Bay to the Gulf of Mexico, Alaska to the Gulf of California.

Sea Robin *(Prionotus evolans):* Common on sandy bottoms from Cape Cod to the Carolinas.

Sea Rocket *(Cakile edentula):* In sandy areas from Southern Labrador to Florida, also along the Great Lakes.

Sea Urchin, Green *(Strongylocentrotus droebachiensis):* On rocky and sandy bottoms from the Arctic to New Jersey, Alaska to Puget Sound.

Seal, Harbor *(Phoca vitulina):* In coastal waters and harbors from the Arctic, Hudson Bay to the Carolinas, south along the Pacific coast.

Shark, Sand *(Mustelus canis):* In the ocean and offshore from the Bay of Fundy along the coast to Cuba.

Skate, Common *(Raja erinacea):* On sandy bottoms in shallow water from Nova Scotia to the Carolinas.

Sponge, Finger *(Haliclona oculata):* On rocks and wood from Labrador to North Carolina.

Squid *(Loligo pealei):* In shallow water during the warm months from the Bay of Fundy to the West Indies.

Starfish, Eastern *(Asterias forbesi):* On rocky and sandy bottoms from Maine to Texas.

Tern, Common *(Sterna hirundo):* Temperate zone of the Northern Hemisphere; winters to the Southern Hemisphere.

Turnstone, Ruddy *(Arenaria interpres):* Along the coast, usually on pebbly beaches and flats in the Arctic and sub-Arctic; circumpolar; winters along the coastal United States, Hawai'i, southern Eurasia to Southern Hemisphere.

Turtle, Green Sea *(Chelonia mydas):* At sea from the New England coast to the West Indies, the Pacific coast north Baja California.

Whale, Humpback *(Megaptera novaeangliae):* Throughout the world's oceans.

Whale, Pilot *(Globicephala melas):* Cool waters on the edge of the continental shelf along the Atlantic coast to Virginia.

Whelk, Knobbed *(Busycon carica):* On sandy and muddy bottoms from Cape Cod to northern Florida; introduced into San Francisco Bay.

Worm, Clam *(Nereis virens):* On sandy and muddy bottoms from Maine to Virginia, the entire Pacific coast.

Worm Shell *(Vermicularia spirata):* On sandy or muddy bottoms from southern Massachusetts to Florida and the West Indies.

Bibliography

Audubon Society Staff and Norman A. Meinkoth. 1981. *Audubon Society Field Guide to North America Seashore Creatures.* New York: Alfred A. Knopf.

Bateman, Graham, ed. 1984. *Sea Mammals—All the World's Animals.* New York: Torstar Books.

Bevans, Micheal H. 1961. *The Book of Sea Shells.* Garden City, N.Y.: Doubleday.

Burton, Robert. 1977. *The Seashore and Its Wildlife.* London: Orbis Publishing.

Burzynski, Michael, and Robert Walker. 1987. *Beach Guide—Fundy National Park.* New Brunswick: Fundy Guild.

Engel, Leonard. 1961. *Life Nature Library—The Sea.* New York: Time-Life Books.

Gordon, N. R. 1990. *Seashells: A Photographic Celebration.* New York: Michael Friedman Publishing Group.

Gosner, Kenneth L. 1978. *A Field Guide to the Atlantic Seashore:* Boston: Houghton Mifflin.

Lawlor, Elizabeth P. 1992. *Discover Nature at the Seashore.* Harrisburg, Pa.: Stackpole Books.

Morris, Percy A. 1951. *A Field Guide to the Shells of the Atlantic and Gulf Coasts.* Boston: Houghton Mifflin.

Miner, Roy W. 1950. *Field Book of Seashore Life.* New York: G. P. Putnam's Sons.

Norman, Marcia G. 1963. *Treasures of the Shore.* Chatham, Mass.: Chatham Conservation Foundation.

Palmer, E. Lawrence. 1949. *Fieldbook of Natural History.* New York: McGraw-Hill.

Parker, Steve. 1989. *Seashore—Eyewitness Books.* New York: Alfred A. Knopf.

Peterson, Roger Tory. 1980. *Field Guide to the Birds—East and Central North America.* Boston: Houghton Mifflin.

Reader's Digest Editors. 1984. *ABC's of Nature.* New York: Reader's Digest Association.

Reader's Digest Editors. 1982. *Joy of Nature.* New York: Reader's Digest Association.

Reader's Digest Editors. 1982. *North American Wildlife.* New York: Reader's Digest Association.

Russell, Franklin. 1975. *The Illustrated Natural History of Canada—The Atlantic Coast.* Toronto, Canada: Natural Science of Canada.

Smith, G. Robin. 1981. *A Guide to the Common Seaweeds of Atlantic Canada.* St. Johns, Newfoundland: Breakwater Books.

Pycraft, W. P., ed. *The Standard Natural History.* Great Britain: Frederick Warne.

Wetmore, Alexander. 1965. *Water Prey and Game Birds of North America.* Washington, D.C.: National Geographic Society.

Zim, Herbert S. 1955. *Seashores.* New York: Simon & Schuster.

MAGAZINES

Ranger Rick. Washington, D.C.: The National Wildlife Federation. Various issues from 1973 to 1993.

National Wildlife Magazine. Washington, D.C.: The National Wildlife Federation. Various issues from 1963 to 1993.

Index

Actitis macularia, 83
Ammophila breviligulata, 104
Anomia simplex, 35
Ardea herodias, 86
Arenaria interpres, 85
Arenicola cristata, 24
Argopecten irradians, 33
Artemisia stelleriana, 98
arthropods, 47
Asterias forbesi, 28–29
Astrangia danae, 22
Aurelia aurita, 20

Balanus balanoides, 56
baleen, 71
barnacle, northern rock, 56
Bay of Fundy, 2–3
bayberry, northern, 102
birds, 75
bladder wrack, 94
blenny, striped, 63
boat shell, 41
book gills, 54–55
bulrush, salt-marsh, 106
burrows, 24–25, 37–39, 53
Busycon carica, 45
butterfish, 64
byssal thread (byssus), 34–35

Cakile edentula, 101
calcium carbonate, 22
Calidris alba, 84
Calidris canutus, 79
Calidris minutilla, 82
camouflage, 59
Cancer irroratus, 50

Cape Cod, 2–3
Cape Hatteras, 2
carapace, 50
Charadrius semipalmated, 80
Chasmodes bosquianus, 63
Chelonia mydas, 68
Chondrus crispus, 92
clam: long-necked, 37; razor, 39; soft-shell, 37
claws, use of, 48, 50–52
coast, rocky, 4, 6–7
coast, sandy, 4
coelenterates, 17
colonies of polyps, 19, 22
coral, northern stony, 22
cordgrass, 105
cormorant, double-crested, 76
crab: fiddler, 51; horseshoe, 54–55; long-clawed hermit, 52; mole, 53; rock, 49; soft-shell, 50
Crassostrea virginica, 36
Crepidula fornicata, 41
Cucumaria frondosa, 31
cunner, 66

dolphin, Atlantic bottlenosed, 73
dulse, 93
dunes. *See* sand dunes
dusty miller, 98

Echinarachnius parma, 30
echinoderms, 26
echolocation, 72–73
eel, common, 64
eelgrass, 103
egg cases, 45–46, 60
Emerita talpoida, 53

Enis directus, 39
exoskeleton, 47, 49
eye placement, 33, 54–55, 59–60, 65
eye spot, 28

fish, 58
fishnets, impacts of, 22, 68, 73
fleas, beach, 57
flounder, 59
foot, of a mollusk, 32, 38–39, 44–45
Fratercula arctica, 87
fronds, 91, 94
Fucus vesiculosus, 94

gills, book, 54–55
glasswort, jointed, 107
Globicephala melas, 72
Gobiosoma bosci, 65
goby, naked, 65
grass, beach, 104
Gulf Stream, vi, 2
gull, herring, 78

habitats, 4–11
Haliclona oculata, 16
heath, beach, 100
heron, great blue, 86
holdfast, 91, 95
Homarus americanus, 48–49
Hudsonia tomentosa, 100

ink, ejecting by squid, 46
intertidal zone, 1

jellyfish, 18–20
jellyfish, moon, 20
jingle shell, 35

kelp, sugar, 95
knot, red, 79

Labrador current, vi, 2
Laminaria saccharina, 95
Larus argentatus, 78
Lathyrus japonicus, 99
limestone, 22
Limonium carolinianum, 108
limpet, tortoise-shell, 40

Limulus polyphemus, 54
Littorina littorea, 42
lobster, 48–49
Loligo pealei, 46
lugworm, 24
Lunatia heros, 44

Maine current, vi
mammals, 69
mantle, 32, 36
Megaptera novaeangliae, 70–71
Mercenaria mercenaria, 38
mermaid's purse, 60
mollusks, 32
molting, 49
moon shell, northern, 44
moss, Irish, 92
mussel, blue, 34
Mustelus canis, 61
Mya arenaria, 37
Myrica pensylvanica, 102
Mytilus edulis, 34

neap tide, 2
nematocysts, 19
Nereis virens, 25
nets. *See* fishnets
Notoacmaea testudinalis, 40

operculum, 41–42, 44–45
oyster, 36

Pagurus longicarpus, 52
Palmaria palmata, 93
pea, beach, 99
pearl oysters, 36
pearls, formation of, 36
peeps, 82
periwinkle, 42
Phalacrocorax auritus, 76
Phoca vitulina, 74
Pholis gunellus, 64
photosynthesis, 91, 93
Physalia physalia, 18–19
pincers, 28
plants: flowering, 97; nonflowering, 91
plover, black-bellied, 81
plover, semipalmated, 80

120

plumage, 75
Pluvialis squatarola, 81
poison, 19, 20
pollution: causing decline in marine life, 22, 68, 73; concentrating in food chain, 25, 34, 37
polyp, 19, 22
pond weed, 103
Portuguese man-of-war, 18–19
Prionotus evolans, 62
proboscis, 45
Pseudopleuronectes americanus, 59
puffin, Atlantic, 87

quahog, northern, 38

radula, 42
Raja erinacea, 60
reefs, 22
rhizomes, 97, 103–5
rocky coast, 4, 6-7
roots, 97. *See also* holdfast; rhizomes

Salicornia europaea, 107
salt marshes, 5, 105–7
sand, composition of, 4
sand bugs, 53
sand collar, 44
sand dollar, 30
sand dunes, 5, 98–100, 102, 104
sand hopper, 57
sanderling, 84
sandpiper, least, 82
sandpiper, spotted, 83
scallop, Atlantic bay, 33
Scirpus robustus, 106
sea anemone, northern red, 21
sea cucumber, orange-footed, 31
sea lavender, 108
sea lettuce, 96
sea robin, 62
sea rocket, 101
sea urchin, green, 27
seagull, 78
seal, harbor, 74
seaweed, 91
shark, sand, 61
shorebirds, 75
siphon, 37–39

skate, common, 60
sieve plate, 28–29
slipper shell, 41
Spartina patens, 105
spines, 27
sponge, finger, 16
sponges, 15–16
spring tide, 2
squid, long-finned, 46
starfish, eastern, 28–29
Sterna hirundo, 77
stinging cells, 19–22
strand line, 4, 8–9
Strongylocentrotus droebachiensis, 27
subtidal zone, 1
suction, by a mollusk foot, 40
suction cups, 46

Talorchestia megalophthalma, 57
Tautogolabrus adspersus, 66
Tealia felina, 21
temperature, of water, 2, 22
tentacles, stinging, 17, 19–22
tern, common, 77
test, 27
tide, 2–4
tide pools, 5, 10–11
tube feet, 26–31
turnstone, ruddy, 85
Tursiops truncatus, 73
turtle, green sea, 68

Uca pugilator, 51
Ulva lactuca, 96

vermicularia spirata, 43

wampum, 38
whale, humpback, 70–71
whale, pilot, 72
whales: breaching of, 71; songs of, 71–72; stranding of, 72
whelk, knobbed, 45
worm shell, 43
worm, clam, 25
worms, 23

Zostera marina, 103

About the Author

PEGGY KOCHANOFF spent summers as a child combing the beaches of Cape Cod. A graduate of Cornell University with a degree in vertebrate zoology, she wrote and illustrated *A Field Guide to Nearby Nature* (Mountain Press, 1994). Her drawings grace the pages of a plant encyclopedia published by Cornell University, brochures distributed by Canada's Department of Lands and Forests, and nature guides. Kochanoff lives in Falmouth, Nova Scotia, where she and her husband operate a tree farm and nursery.